Sierra
Story

Sierra Story

▲

Yosemite Adventures & Reflections

▲

Henry B. Stark

Henry B. Stark (signature)

Southfarm Press, Publisher
Middletown, Connecticut

All of the hiking experiences described in this book happened as written, but the major characters, aside from the author, his wife Cher, John Lazzeri, and David and Liz Lovegrove are all imaginary. No reference is intended to any other real person, living or dead, except for the historical characters mentioned. The major geography is actual, the minor geography as near as actual as the author can remember. Geographical and historical changes may have overtaken ones that the author has described.

Copyright © 2000 by Henry B. Stark

Publishing Imprint of Haan Graphic Publishing Services, Ltd.
Box 1296, Middletown, Connecticut 06457

ISBN: 0-913337-39-0
▲
Library of Congress Cataloging-in-Publication Data
Stark, Henry B., 1937-
  Sierra story : Yosemite adventures & reflections / Henry B. Stark.
    p.   cm.
  Includes bibliographical references and index.
  ISBN 0-913337-39-0 (alk. paper)
  1. Backpacking—Sierra Nevada (Calif. And Nev.) 2. Backpacking—
Yosemite National Park (Calif.) 3. Stark, Henry B., 1937---Journeys—
Sierra Nevada (Calif. And Nev.) 4. Stark, Henry B., 1937---Journeys—
Yosemite National Park (Calif.) I. Title: Yosemite adventures &
reflections. II. Title.

GV 199.42.S55 S82 2000
917.94'470453—dc21
                                                    00-040002

▲
Every effort has been made to locate the copyright holders of all copyrighted materials and to secure the necessary permissions to reproduce them. In the event of any questions arising as to their use, the author will make necessary changes in future printings.

Printed in the United States of America

Visit *Sierra Story*'s website at: http://www.sierrastory.com

She is the closest a human can come to being a corporeal Angel on earth. She loves everyone, completely and unconditionally. Effortlessly, she has consecrated herself to living a selfless life in the service of others. I recently posed a hypothetical question; if she knew for certain that she would die in exactly one year, how would she spend her time? Her response, "I would get on the phone and tell as many people that I knew that I loved them and try to provide shelter for as many homeless people as I could."

She is unfailingly optimistic, extremely intelligent, gentle, and has the best sense of humor I have ever encountered. Her daily life is a perfect blend and balance of the spiritual, emotional, mental, and physical. We met eons ago in a past life and I was blessed to encounter her again in this incarnation. This time she is my wife and my best friend. While I wrote this book she supplied unlimited encouragement, patiently endured my incessant and obsessive chatter, and served as editor-in-chief. With the fullest of hearts,

I dedicate this book to Cher.

▲

I'd like to thank Anna Quindlen.
Without her personal encouragement
I would not have written this book.

H.B.S.

"The earth doesn't belong to us —
we belong to the earth."

—Chief Seattle,
1854

Part 1
Friends

One

    As the plane carried me through the darkness that separated New York from Los Angeles, I couldn't release the thoughts that had plagued me for weeks. How can Tomoko, Jon and I spend 15 days in the remotest areas of Yosemite National Park given the events of the past 15 months? With their history of serious marital problems and their bizarre and revolting request for my intervention, it almost appeared as if I was being set up for a personal disaster instead of a carefree vacation.

    How uncomfortable would it be for us to be so close to each other in such intimate surroundings? After all, we would be sleeping near each other, washing and bathing in the open and there were no toilet facilities on our route. In addition, there would be the normal opportunities for social interactions during the day—through the rigors of hiking, the relief of breaks, the conversations around campfires.

I looked out the window and watched as the blackness was occasionally interrupted by small clusters of shimmering lights passing below. I wondered if most of the homes down there housed families that were dysfunctional to some extent. If they did, then dysfunction had become the norm. I wondered how the so-called experts measure varying degrees of normalcy versus dysfunction? I had never heard of anyone in my circle of friends being put into the dilemma that I had been.

I couldn't get it out of my head that several months earlier Jon and Tomoko had made their shocking proposal and even though I had forcefully turned them down, it still seemed to hang in the air. In fact, as many years as we might continue to be friends, it would always be an issue for me.

I learned later that Jon had spent considerable time and effort trying to convince his wife that their marriage pattern had left her in a state of depression and that she needed an emotional stimulant. Since I had been their trusted friend for many years, I could be relied on to provide the fulfillment she needed without being a threat to their marriage.

As a national sales manager for a large men's

sportswear company it had been my responsibility to travel around the country and work with each of my thirty salespeople. When I needed to spend time with my Los Angeles man, I always planned to complete the territory by Friday. Jon and Tomoko asked me, on many occasions, to be a sounding board for them. I had no training, but they were close friends and I was deeply committed to helping their marriage survive. With the weekends free and ending up in their neck of the woods, I spent time listening to each of them. Then I brought them together hoping to bridge their ever widening communication gaps. When they were with me one on one, each was candid and each was angry. But when the three of us were together it was terribly difficult getting them to express true emotions and use direct language. We did make significant progress as time went on but I was dealing with two very different people with backgrounds and value systems that would never meet.

Having recently been divorced myself, I was in no mood to become entangled in a new relationship. In fact, the last stages of my marriage and the divorce process had been so mean-spirited that I had vowed never to marry again.

There was no romantic involvement between Tomoko and me. I liked her in a very special way and felt sorry for what she had to put up with in her day-to-day dealings with Jon. You could say that I loved her as I love everyone when I am in touch with my spiritual self. I thoroughly enjoyed her company, respected her sharp mind, looked forward to spending time with her and wanted her to be as happy as possible. We had shared many significant moments. Sometimes I thought of her as my sister, sometimes my friend.

When I was married, Jonathan and Tomoko Roberts had been our best friends. We did almost everything together. We had a lot in common, such as playing tennis, cards and cooking. We even had our children at about the same times before we met. After my divorce I maintained a strong relationship with them. My ex-wife dropped out of the picture, but the picture itself became more awkward, because a single friend with an unhappily married couple can create restiveness.

Our society doesn't encourage threesomes. When we're thrown into the stew of relationships, we don't tend to think of our own in societal terms. We believe that ours is different from the norm and that we have the necessary insight and tools to make it work. Through rationalization, we convince ourselves that we have the unique ability to create successful and fulfilling relationships even if others don't. And because of our self-delusion, we often end up making a mess of them. At that point it is extremely hard to restore constructive lines of communications between the married couple and with the single person who may look and feel like an unwelcome intruder.

Tomoko, Jon, and I were comfortable in any combination. I was always happy to be with either of them. But when Jon first suggested that I have a sexual relationship with Tomoko, I was shocked. I immediately said no. The idea horrified me. I had never thought of Tomoko in that way. The whole idea seemed destructive. I had difficulty comprehending how this could help their marriage. It seemed that Jon wanted to drive a wedge through it and I had no desire to be the wedge. Because we lived on opposite coasts and didn't see each other often, the idea was tabled for many months, although I gave it lots of thought between visits to California.

I tried to imagine Jon dealing with the "saving the marriage" issue. This was actually more difficult for me to understand. Their relationship was already on the rocks and getting worse. They were fighting openly in front of their children and friends. It seemed that mutual respect had disappeared. In my mind, at that time, there was no doubt that divorce was imminent. My problem was understanding how this particular action on my part might help them. They had both assured me that this was, at the very least, a positive start for them and at best, might spur them into action with a professional counselor. They were urging me, virtually begging me, to help them save their union. I knew that marriage counselors sometimes advocated sexual surrogates for some of their patients. Why didn't Jon and Tomoko get one of them instead of asking me!

But even though I rejected the idea of having a sexual relationship with Tomoko, I couldn't rein in my active imagination. I tried to imagine a physical relationship with Tomoko. What would it be like? What would someone who was so quiet and submissive in daily relationships be like in the privacy of the bedroom away from her husband? Having been married for 14 years and living monogamously, I felt uncomfortable with the idea of exploring relationships with other women. My new-found legal and moral freedom hadn't yet inscribed itself into my consciousness.

I had always been backward in this regard. My parents had transferred me to an all boys' school in the fifth grade and during my formative pubescent years I had had little contact with girls. I had always been uncomfortable with them and felt inadequate in social situations. When my school invited a girls' school to a Friday night dance, I could always be found along the wall of the gymnasium, talking with several other insecure boys. I never had to deal with rejection because I never dared to put myself in rejection's way by asking a girl to dance. I was convinced that I had nothing to offer girls my age. Now, many years later, I was being handed a lovely and willing woman on a silver platter.

Being with Tomoko was comfortable. Could having sex with her could help me bridge the gap between my ex-wife and the formidable array of unknown women who were "out there" in what my friends and the press sometimes referred to as "the meat market". Besides, my self-confidence needed as much bracing as possible. I was sure that having been with one woman for so long, I had formed a comfortable, routine, behavioral pattern that might not be accepted by the new generation of experienced women I was planning to meet and hoped to date. I simply didn't remember the old courting procedures, plus I knew they must have modernized to rituals I never had learned and wouldn't recognize. I would be extremely nervous about finding myself in a bedroom setting with anyone other than my wife. I was out of touch, out of the loop, and very anxious. Although Tomoko could never be the one to ease me back into the dating world, the episode made me wonder if I should be looking for a single woman somewhere else.

As the plane flew on, I thought about how Tomoko viewed sex. She had been used to being taken advantage of and thought good sex was doing anything necessary to satisfy Jon. If he had an orgasm, she had done her job. I wouldn't be surprised if I learned that she thought the average sexual experience took 3.6 minutes. When she grew up as the youngest of four sisters with a dominating father, she had been taught, and learned the lesson well, that the woman's needs were irrelevant. For his part, Jon looked at sex as a necessary, periodic physical release and when the release had been achieved, he was quickly off to his next activity.

I was a married man during the previous vacation with Jon and Tomoko, a rafting trip down the Tuolumne River also in Yosemite National Park. My wife was not a devotee of prolonged and strenuous outdoor activities. Her idea of an outdoor adventure was a couple of sets of tennis followed by a trip to the ice-cream store. We had invited her along but she declined and graciously urged me to go alone. She knew how much I enjoyed extended camping trips in unspoiled natural settings.

To avoid the uncomfortable threesome scenario, Jon had invited his sister along to make it a foursome. Having never met Jean, I was wary of spending 15 days with her. If we didn't get on well there was no place to go. We would just have to stick it out until we got back to civilization. At least there were other people along on that trip. The river was endangered and in order to protect it from erosion, trash and other human insults, trips down the Tuolumne were regulated. We went with about a dozen other rafters and a licensed guide. Actually Jean and I got along well and I was glad she had joined us. I enjoyed the harmless flirting and felt safe knowing that she was aware that I was married.

The trip I was headed for this year was going to be entirely different. There would just be the three of us and we planned to tackle some very difficult terrain in remote wilderness. If we had any kind of conflict, there would be no bailout point. I wondered if Jon and I would have a problem because I had flatly turned down his request. Would he bring it up again? The last thing I wanted was a confrontation around an evening campfire, but I felt reasonably secure that Jon would never ask me again.

These kinds of thoughts made the six hour plane trip literally fly by.

As I pushed up my little shade and looked out the window, I noticed that the clusters of lights below were larger, nearer, and much brighter. We were approaching Los Angeles.

As we descended I wondered if my backpack, checked by the airline, would arrive intact, in tatters or at all. And how would it be to see Tomoko—and Jon?

It turned out to be wonderful to be met at the

Los Angeles airport by my friends. We hugged each other spontaneously and were genuinely happy to see each other. It was a major relief, ten minutes later, to see my bright orange backpack serpentining on the baggage conveyer belt. An hour later we were at their home enjoying a welcoming drink. Being with Jon and Tomoko again felt comfortable and easy. My anxieties dissolved in the cognac. We were all so excited about the up-coming two weeks that we talked long into the night about supplies, equipment, proposed routes, and other trip details. Despite the three-hour time change and the long travel day, I felt no fatigue.

Two

After breakfast the next morning we planned the meals for the trip. I really enjoyed this part. We were looking to put together meals that were tasty, nutritious, and light-weight and this proved to be a problem. We decided to avoid the prepackaged meals sold by outdoor stores. They were too expensive, had too many artificial ingredients and sounded completely unappetizing. We didn't want meal time to be a time to dread. Stopping along the trail to eat was supposed to be something to look forward to. We settled on buying packages of dried fruit, nuts, and cereal. We carefully calculated the number of meals we would be eating over the course of the hike then added a few extras for snacks and emergencies in case we didn't get back in time.

Watching Tomoko at work was fun. She placed 15 large bowls on counters and tables around the kitchen. Then she opened a box of dried apricots and put one apricot into each bowl. She made sure that each bowl, or lunch, had one piece of fruit before she continued emptying the box. Next came the pears, raisins, almonds, cashews, peanuts and M&M's. No lunch was to have more than any other. Finally we added some vitamin enriched, lightly sugared, dry cereal. The last step was to divide each day's lunch into three small Ziploc bags for individual portions. We felt very smug about how efficient and economical we had been.

We did use the outdoor store for items such as light-weight cooking pots, Sterno cans, and things we needed but couldn't purchase elsewhere. Back at the house we tried to evenly divide all of our clothing, cookware, food, and personal gear making allowance for Tomoko's lighter weight and smaller frame. A bathroom scale came in handy. After we weighed ourselves without packs we kept stepping on and off with the packs in an attempt to evenly distribute the loads. Jon and I ended up with 55 pounds, Tomoko a bit less. My friend John Lazzeri, who has hiked the entire length of the Appalachain Trail from Georgia to Maine, more than 2,000 miles, now tells me he never takes more than 40 pounds with him and he's always in great physical shape. My training for this 15 day, basically uphill hike through some of America's most rugged country was jogging in sneakers around a flat high school track two to five miles a day. It had never even occurred to me that we would be starting our trek at just under 5,000 feet in elevation and would be working our way up to 9,000 feet. The air would be thinner and our breathing would be labored under normal conditions. In looking back at my thinking, I can only say, "color me stupid."

Jon and Tomoko went shopping for personal items during that afternoon. Left alone in their house, my eyes focused on their living room pictures. I soon fell into a reverie about my two friends and their personalities and values.

Jon was a Scorpio who should have been born a Gemini. He had two distinct personas. To his colleagues he was a serious intellectual, totally focused on his profession. He taught courses like Economic Evaluation of Capital Investment Projects and Introduction to Derivative Securities at the business school of a prestigious West Coast university. Jon had proudly shown me his curriculum vitae with three pages of journal articles and research reports he had written over 25 years. He had also collaborated on a number of books, and I had devoted part of a bookshelf to his complimentary copies that arrived with warm, personal inscriptions. I couldn't begin to comprehend any of these tomes but I valued the fact that I knew an author and that he had written me personal notes inside his books. They still sit there, gathering dust.

If I wanted to be charitable I would say that Jon was an ordinary teacher. He thought of teaching as a necessary evil that must be performed in order to earn him an office, a computer, a salary, and tenure. Given an option, he would gladly have devoted all of his time to research and increasing the length of his publishing record. He had an active disdain for faculty colleagues who loved the classroom and were good teachers. He classified them at the lowest level of the academic totem pole. That's one of the many disagreements I had with him. I could not see the point of a lot of purely theoretical research, but I surely appreciated good teaching. I was inspired by good teachers and they changed the direction of my life. I'm also happy that a number of my students have told me that it was enlightening to learn from my Ethics modules, that it was possible to have a successful career and make a good living while staying true to one's own values. I have seen how one good teacher can inspire a lifetime of study, be responsible for career-path changes, or encourage the development and maintenance of moral principles. Having taught part-time for over 20 years, I know that I have made a difference in a number of my students' lives and I consider this a major accomplishment.

Away from the university Jon was a totally different person. He had a very expensive Japanese-made camera with lots of lenses. I know he paid more for one telephoto lens than I have paid for all the photographic equipment I've owned over my lifetime. He needed a powerful lens so that he could clearly see naked women sunbathing and playing on nude beaches. He seemed to have a deep-seated need to be around younger women and the more naked they were the better. Unfortunately this passion had prompted him to seduce a number of his research assistants. He had shown me dozens of pictures of them in a wide variety of seductive poses in various stages of undress. I really couldn't abide his having affairs, any affairs. Worse yet, he did it with work colleagues, and still worse, his own subordinates. Tomoko, who knew about his photography but not his sexual extra-curricular activities, tolerated his hobby and professed pride in his talent. Personally I think she was either in denial or blithely ignorant of the possible consequences.

I have to admit that I am glad that Jon had this hobby because I used it as a cover under which to hide my curiosity. I did enjoy going to the beach with him and having an excuse for being around his female subjects. He approached them with his camera hanging around his neck, (he was often nude when he did this), and told them how attractive or sensual or interesting or provocative or... they were and asked if he could take a picture. He further used the occasion to ask for an address so he could send along some complimentary prints. He was smooth, and they often agreed. I'm amazed at how easy it was for him and how he emitted an air of legitimacy. I didn't want to know what happened after that and I didn't ask, but on subsequent visits to his home office I had seen pictures of women we had met on the beach displayed along his walls. I doubt if the same friendly, naked women if dressed, would so welcome an approach by a male stranger in a more formal environment, for example, in their business offices. Do we have different sets of values for different facets and times of our lives? Are we like chameleons who change personas to fit in with our different environments?

I admired Jon's photographic talent and his chutzpah, but I thought of him as a dirty old man who cheated on his wife.

Jon had been my friend over the years not because of emotional sharing but because I had been starved for people with whom I could explore ideas. My work colleagues and neighbors were more interested in discussing soap operas and sports results than thoughts and opinions. Jon actually hated any show of emotion and was incapable of it himself. He visibly winced when I put an arm around him when someone once took our picture together. Jon was probably the only friend I had that I didn't routinely hug upon meeting and leaving. I think one of the reasons Tomoko was so dull around him was that she had learned how much he appreciated cold, calculating unemotional efficiency.

I have a strong intellectual curiosity, and Jon and I could spend hours and hours discussing and arguing about various issues. One of the topics that we had explored at length was our view of an ideal marriage.

Jon looked at marriage as an economic model, a practical solution to economic problems. He believed there need not be, in fact there shouldn't be, an emotional sharing. Showing or even having emotion of any kind was unmanly and a waste of energy, according to him. He looked at it strictly from the husband's point of view: He had needs and the wife had needs and the two should work together to satisfy those needs as fairly and as amicably as possible. If the wife had to sacrifice a bit more than the husband, well, that's in the nature of things.

Jon divided his needs into two major categories, work and sex.

His ideas on marital sex could be quickly described. Tomoko should be available whenever he wanted her. Her own feelings and needs were irrelevant. The expression "wham, bam, thank you ma'am" could have been invented for guys like Jon. I learned from Tomoko that she did, in fact, think that each sexual encounter should last about 3.6 minutes. That's all she had ever known. If you've only been with one man how can you make a comparison? I wonder how many women have been brought up to believe that they have a duty to satisfy their men and that their own needs and desires are not important. I think that the myth some men have perpetrated on women is shameful. As far as I know, Tomoko had never experienced an orgasm with a man and I know that she never thought she was missing anything.

She probably had no idea what foreplay, cuddling, and caressing were all about. For her, sex with Jon must have seemed like "hurry up or I'll miss my bus".

Jon also expected Tomoko to fulfill his work requirements in a very basic way. She should shop for his clothes, wash and iron them and lay them out for him each morning. Appetizing food should be in the refrigerator at all times and dinner should be on the table a half hour after he came home from work. They did do the dishes together. When Jon wanted to invite visiting international professors or colleagues to dinner, Tomoko was expected to plan the meals and prepare them, soup to nuts. Jon's responsibility was to obtain and keep a job and supply the money to keep the household running. It was a cold and calculating economic arrangement. It makes me sad to think that there are many marriages like that in the world.

Tomoko accepted all of this without complaint. They had three children and to her nothing was more important than being a super mom. Arguing with or complaining to Jon was counterproductive to that goal. When he wanted sex, she complied; when he wanted a dinner party, she provided. As the youngest of four sisters, she had so suppressed herself that she always seemed quiet and on the verge of depression. Several times a day people asked her, "Are you okay?" I have lots of pictures of Jon and Tomoko and she's not smiling in any of them.

Just as Jon had different personalities at work and in private life, so did Tomoko. As a child she was very involved with pets. There were always dogs and cats in her household and she took it upon herself to take care of them. With parents who dispensed love only on a conditional basis, she thrived on the unconditional love of her animals. It was only natural that after majoring in zoology in college that she gravitated to combining science with animals in her career.

She had assisted veterinarians in her spare time in both high school and college. In addition to performing mundane clerical tasks, she obtained some valuable hands-on experience giving vaccinations, drawing blood, taking and developing x-rays, and assisting in surgeries on an assortment of dogs, cats, birds, snakes, and ferrets.

After graduation from college she earned her Doctor of Veterinary Medicine degree at a prestigious upstate New York university. Her comprehensive background enabled her to quickly obtain a job with a leading veterinary practice when she returned to California. There she progressed from performing minor surgeries such as neutering, spaying, and declawing cats to major operations such as repairing hips and knees on dogs.

Because of her quiet competence and because she had complete control of her technical skills, she commanded a great deal of personal respect from the three vets who ran the office. The technicians she was soon supervising respected her and felt they were her partners rather than her subordinates.

She now owned her own practice in suburban Los Angeles. I think that the certified veterinary technician, office manager, kennel keeper, and groomers who worked there adored her. On my visits to her clinic, it was amazing for me to see how secure she was with herself at work and how docile and submismissive she was at home.

Away from Jon she had a real personality.

I always looked forward to sitting down with Tomoko and talking. She was interesting and involved. As a scientist, she had a wonderfully astute way of analyzing the world. She was kind and sympathetic and always spoke well of everyone. I'll never forget the time we had a long conversation about sex. She disclaimed an interest in it saying that what was important to her was love, warmth, and acceptance. A good cuddle was much more welcome than intercourse. She longed for a relationship where she could be valued for herself, who she was, not what she did. She wanted to hear heartfelt words of love said with sincere feeling. While I listened to her and looked into her eyes, I felt a sadness and frustration that such a wonderful person was so unhappy. After we go through all the dating games and finally find a spouse, we are supposed to live happily ever after. (I learned that from fairy tales and marketers.) While Tomoko talked I thought that she was expressing the views of many women. It's a shame she got tied up with Jon. There have to be many sensitive men looking for someone like her. I really liked Tomoko and Jon individually, and I liked being with them as a couple, but that didn't change the fact that they had a lousy marriage.

We met many years ago through our kids. We

were neighbors and they had three children who enjoyed playing with our two children. It was convenient to have each other as built-in baby sitters who were so easily accessible. Eventually my wife and I divorced. I always thought that Jon and Tomoko should have divorced too but I know it would have interfered with their concept of an economically efficient marriage. Jon once explained to me, with numbers, charts, and tables, that two people living separately could never manage as cheaply as two people sharing the same house. This maxim overruled any wishes for personal fulfillment. There was no room for love in any of his computations.

My children suffered greatly because my first wife and I got divorced—theirs suffered because they didn't.

Which brings up the subject of why have children. I am acquainted with couples who believe that in order to fulfill their marriage they must have children. There is a common belief that we exist in order to propagate the human race and, if one is married and lives a childless life, it has been a life of failure. One may be exonerated if there is a physical impediment that prevents conception.

If a couple is physically capable and chooses not to have children, it can present a moral dilemma. Friends of mine who live below the so-called poverty line would like to have children but feel they shouldn't. If they are unable to provide a desirable standard of living to their progeny, they believe they have a responsibility not to bring children into the world.

I also have homosexual friends in long-term childless relationships who are convinced that they are living fulfilled and complete lives. This is a complex subject and I am loath to make judgments, but I would like to draw a semantic distinction. I believe couples who would like to have children and can't should be considered childless. Couples who can have children but decide not to are child free.

The planet doesn't need a larger population. But Jon Roberts felt that if you don't provide your fair share of children, you are not exercising your responsibility. I believe not having children may have a positive impact depending on your circumstances and where you are living.

Some of my friends spend more time and effort researching automobiles they contemplate purchasing than whether or not to have children. There would be a great deal more personal fulfillment by all involved if more time were spent on this subject.

Whether they have children or not, one of the hardest decisions many married couples have to make is: Should we get divorced and if so when? So many pundits appear on television talk shows, each giving advice that is too general and simplistic.

Graphics appear on the screen as if we need only to buy their book or copy down their four rules or eight steps to instantly solve our own problems. I never took a course on marriage and I never had contemplated the idea of divorce, that was for the other fifty percent of married couples. I just did the best I could in everyday situations. So did my wife. It wasn't enough. We debated for three debilitating years whether or not we should stay together. What's the best thing for the kids?

In retrospect I think kids do better in a home with love and harmony whether or not the parents are separated. If the parents can't get along, fight all the time, and can't reconcile their differences, it's probably better to separate and remove the cause of the friction. Staying together until the children reach a certain, arbitrarily selected, age is damaging to everyone. We are all constantly growing and changing and it's important to respect one's partner enough to let him or her grow in whatever direction is best and to be there with love and support. If possessiveness or jealousy are a problem, perhaps one was not ready for marriage in the first place. I like the sparrow story. When you display your open palm the sparrow alights. If you try to close your hand to capture it, it flees. If I encourage my wife to grow and develop in her own way at her own pace I don't think she'll want to fly away. When I got married the first time I was too young to know if I had established any of my own values and if I had, what they were. I just wanted to be on my own, independent of my family. I married for all the wrong reasons. To me, marriage is not an economic contract. You should assure yourself, as much as possible, that you will want to be with your partner all your life, all the while remembering that you're the last person qualified to make an objective judgment.

Now, in my second marriage, my wife and I work hard to spend time with each other. We share a mutual respect and deep-seated love and like to do many things together. We enjoy hiking, tennis, theater, music, dining, traveling, and on and on. Few moments pass without us talking or laughing. We believe that open and honest communication and a sense of humor are the best possible qualities to have in a marriage. Our sex is more loving and caring and actually better than ever.

But as much as we enjoy being together, we encourage each other to be fulfilled by engaging in separate activities. We recognize that we are different people with different interests. We want each other to be happy and understand that we can't supply all of each other's needs. We understand that we can't be a happy and fulfilled couple if we're not happy and fulfilled individuals.

Apparently Jon and Tomoko didn't share the same philosophy. They could not wait to go to work

each morning. They dreaded spending time together. They had less and less in common the older
their children got. I saw them filling their weekends
with social events to avoid having to be together
alone. Dinner parties, card games, athletic events
bridged the gap from Friday to Monday. They found
excuses to work on Saturdays. If they saw a Friday or
Saturday night coming along with nothing planned
they called friends or colleagues and invited them
over for dinner. For them a loveless marriage was
more economically efficient than managing two
separate households. I don't think either of them
wanted to contemplate the idea of being single again
and going through the dating rituals with all the
inherent insecurities and rejections. The devil they
knew was better than the devil they didn't know.

Before my divorce the four of us spent an
incredible percentage of our social life together. We
were the couple they called to help them fill their
down time. We planned our vacations to be at the
same place at the same time. I've noticed that it is
very rare for a married couple to retain a relationship
with both members of a divorced couple. After my
divorce I remained friends with Jon and Tomoko. We
continued to plan our vacations together, only as a
threesome. The Yosemite trip was just an extension of
the previous years' vacations, only this time I knew it
would be very different.

Three

Look at a map of California and about 300 miles north of Los Angeles you'll see a green irregular oblong-type blotch labeled Yosemite National Park. The land area is about 1,200 square miles but a huge majority of the four million tourists who visit annually, and ninety-percent of those who stay overnight, crowd into a seven-mile-long by one-mile-wide valley. Yosemite Valley is the place where you see such famous geological features as El Capitan, Half Dome, Bridal Veil Falls, Glacier Point, and Vernal Falls. Unfortunately it's also a place where you can get your car repaired at a garage, visit innumerable gift shops, be affronted by gaudy concessionaire signs, buy liquor, stay in several hotels, and mail a letter at a post office. There is even a jail.

I've visited Yosemite National Park about a half dozen times and never been to Yosemite Valley. I'm content to admire Ansel Adams' photographs and let my imagination color in the rest. For me, the other 1,200 square miles is the attraction. I prefer the company of the many deer, bears, and coyotes in the park to the loud, inconsiderate humans and their foul smelling, noisy vehicles. In camping and hiking, I am always attracted by Robert Frost's maxim, "Two roads diverged in a wood, and I—I took the one less traveled by, and that has made all the difference."

Ansel Adams' photographic studies of Yosemite have brought it to the attention of many who will never have the opportunity to visit it. He actually took his first photo of Yosemite in 1916 with a Brownie box camera when he was only 14 years old.

I can't mention Ansel Adams without giving credit to John Muir. Muir, one could safely say, was almost single-handedly responsible for Yosemite's preservation. Born in Scotland in 1838, he came to the United States ten years later. He spent much of his life lobbying Presidents Benjamin Harrison and Theodore Roosevelt to set aside the Yosemite area and give it government protection. The 1890 legislation designating Yosemite a national park was a direct consequence of Muir's efforts.

Teddy Roosevelt arranged a trip to Yosemite

in 1903, anxious to see the grandeur that others had described. After arriving there, he turned down all the pomp and circumstance that had been planned and elected to spend three days and nights hiking and camping with Muir. After three days of exposure to Muir's uninterrupted lobbying, Roosevelt returned to Washington and proposed to congress that the whole area, including Yosemite Valley and the Mariposa Grove of sequoia trees, be joined into a national park. It was. In 1892, Muir had founded the Sierra Club which is still very active in helping preserve America's natural areas. I particularly like one of the quotes attributed to Muir, "The winds will blow their own freshness into you and the storms their energy." Both Adams and Muir have national forests named for them in the area.

The three of us, Tomoko, Jon, and I, had visited Yosemite several times in the past for hiking and rafting vacations. We had been in isolated areas and had rarely seen other hikers. This solitude always left us with the feeling that we were the first humans to enjoy Yosemite's rugged beauty.

But human beings were in the Yosemite area long before even Adams and Muir. Artifacts uncovered indicate that hunter-gatherers lived there as early as 1,400 B.C. They were called Miwoks, and they named the area *Ahwahnee*, "the place of the big mouth", a reference to the shape of the valley. They called themselves *Ahwahneechee*, "the people of that place." We know that they built conical homes and created villages of various public houses.

The first white men to enter the valley were probably frontiersmen who passed through around 1833. In 1839, John Sutter obtained some land in California, which later became known as Sutter's Fort, at the convergence of the American and Sacramento Rivers. He built a sawmill at the sight. In 1848, James Marshall, a carpenter, discovered gold in the American River by Sutter's Mill. The American River is actually composed of three major forks that flow toward, what is now, Sacramento. All of the branches source their water from snowmelt from the mountains surrounding Lake Tahoe.

One year after the gold discovery, the gold rush was in full force. This signaled the beginning of the end of the peace and solitude of California in general, and Yosemite in particular.

Miners and prospectors arrived by horse-drawn stage coaches. Stores to service the miners were constructed and quickly grew into boom towns. James Savage, an ex-prospector, owned such a store that was raided by Indians in 1850. The governor of the new state of California appointed Savage a major in the army and charged him with the responsibility of leading a voluntary cavalry militia into the mountains to round up the Indians and lead them to a reservation well away from the area. The so-called Mariposa Battalion set out in March 1851. On March 27, before they found the Indians, the soldiers came upon the Yosemite Valley at a place we now call Inspiration Point. Though awed by its beauty and majesty, the battalion remained undeterred from its mission.

It's amazing how suddenly and swiftly the valley changed. In 1851, it was known only to, and inhabited by, Indians. In 1855, the *Ahwahnee* were gone and the tourists started arriving. The word *Yosemite* derives from the Miwok word for "the Indians who lived in the valley," or the "yo'hem-iteh." The Miwoks lived on the western side of the valley and the Paiutes on the east. After surviving there for thousands of years, the yo'hem-iteh were evicted in only four.

By the 1870s the destruction of the park was well under way. Loggers were clear-cutting the forests, leaving behind fields of stumps; miners were diverting rivers and leveling hills as they blasted their way through granite to uncover precious gold. They found nuggets that weighed as much as 20 pounds. The gold dust they panned in the river had an immediate market value of $18 an ounce.

A railroad was needed to bring people and supplies in and out, so a large swath was cut for the Central Pacific Railroad. It was built between 1863 and 1868. Engineers planning the route decided to blast fifteen tunnels through the mountains to make a pathway for the tracks. To protect the trains and the tracks from the many avalanches that occurred in winter, they constructed forty miles of wood-covered snow sheds for the trains to pass under. Miners used high-pressure water hoses to destroy the hills and cliffs and pulverize them into dust. Those hoses were so powerful that if a man was within two hundred feet of one, and got hit by the water, it could kill him.

The Paiute term *Inyo* meant, "the dwelling place of a great spirit." The white men were making a mockery of Inyo.

Nowadays the minors, prospectors, and rail-road construction crews are gone. In their place we see motley crowds of tourists arriving in the park. In high season, Memorial Day to Labor Day, cars, trucks, SUVs, and recreational vehicles of all descriptions and sizes line up, sometimes for hours, at the four main entrances. Park rangers have been known to refuse entry to 10,000 vehicles a year. There just isn't room for everyone who wants to gawk, take photos, buy souvenirs, and tramp about the seven square mile valley. Unfortunately the exhaust from the vehicles that do gain admittance is trapped by the mountains and hangs in the valley, obscuring the view and choking the lungs.

When I visit Yosemite I drive to an almost unknown, little used fifth entrance, the Hetch Hetchy. Hetch Hetchy is named for the natural food prepared by the original inhabitants of the valley, the Miwok and Paiute Indians.

This is where Tomoko, Jon, and I would go in two days. The Hetch Hetchy entrance is lightly used because you can't drive through the park like you can at the other entrances. This road dead-ends. I am immediately plunged into the most beautiful and natural scenery imaginable: uplifted granite mountains scoured by wind, rain and snow; smooth glass-like glacial lakes; unspoiled rivers; and an amazing variety of wild flowers and trees. I like it just the way it is, rugged, natural, quiet. To my mind the green, irregular oblong blotch on the map represents two separate and distinct parks, Yosemite Valley and everything else.

Since we had pretty much completed the preparations for the hike, we thought it would be fun and relaxing to go to Jon's favorite nude beach near San Diego on Saturday. It was a welcome break for me after months of particularly stressful work in New York. We arrived at the beach early, in time to stake out a smooth patch of sand well above the high tide line. Soon the beach was full of blankets and naked bodies representing a wide panoply of sizes and shapes.

I noticed that with Tomoko along, Jon had not

brought his camera. I thought to myself, since he takes nude beach photos when she's not there and displays them on the walls of their home, why doesn't he bring his camera when she's present? She has a lovely figure but I've not seen photos of her nude. Lots of photographers have taken and displayed pictures of their wives and girl friends. I also wonder if he's embarrassed to go through his "approaching naked ladies he doesn't know" routine with Tomoko looking on? I'm pretty sure I know the answer to that one. I don't want to bring up an issue that could be counter productive to my amateur marriage counseling, but I wonder if Tomoko has made the connection that there are pictures of nude women, taken by her husband, in her home, but he never has his camera when she goes with him. If she has realized this, I'd be interested in learning her conclusions.

Being nude is wonderful when it's under the warm sun with other people who also feel comfortable about their bodies. There were only two problems. One, I never got used to the men on the cliffs looking down on the beach with binoculars and photo lenses, and two, I stayed in the sun too long and burned areas of my body that would later be called upon to support the hip strap of my very heavy backpack.

Sunday and Monday we did our last-minute

shopping, route planning, and food packaging. We planned a total hike of 45 miles in 15 days, thereby giving ourselves lots of time to enjoy the countryside. After all, this was our vacation, not a forced march. We reassured ourselves that we were already in shape and that as we went along we would only grow stronger.

The food from the supermarket came in heavy jars and cans so we removed it and combined it with the freeze-dried, pre-packaged camping food from the sporting goods store. The supermarket food was significantly cheaper than the specialty food, so we didn't mind the extra work. Indulging ourselves, we stopped at the liquor store on the way home to buy some brandy for "medicinal purposes" on cold Sierra nights and poured it into a very unappetizing plastic bottle.

We cut the excess foil from the packets, combined all the dried ingredients, took the sealed envelopes out of soup boxes and discarded the boxes. We added instant dry milk to some of the dry cereal. At breakfast time on the trail we would add water to the cereal and it would, we hoped, taste like we were in our own home. For treats we threw in some candy bars and small packages of cheese.

It's interesting to contrast our food preparation for Yosemite with that of the early Miwoks. They gathered acorns from under the many black oak trees, mashed them to a pulp, cooked the mash on hot rocks and ate it. It was a staple of their diet and provided the necessary energy to perform their strenuous daily tasks. The acorns were so vital to their economy and well-being that every village had at least one acorn storage center.

By Tuesday morning all of our equipment and food had been split up and distributed and our packs were ready. We made a list of all the equipment we were carrying and in whose pack we had put it. Each of us took a copy of the list so we knew what the other was bringing in the way of community equipment and personal clothing. I carried a lightweight seventy percent down sleeping bag, foam sleeping pad, and a two-man tent. Jon and Tomoko were determined to sleep outdoors regardless of the weather so they dispensed with a tent. They liked the idea of sleeping under the stars. It was also an item of weight that they could avoid carrying. It would take only two nights on the trail for them to realize what a big mistake they had made. I had purchased new hiking boots, waterproofed them, and thought I had done a thorough job of breaking them in back in suburban New York.

Our organizing was done to the finest detail, including putting wooden matches in three different screwtop, waterproof pill vials. We carried codein tablets, antibiotics, aspirin, cold remedies, and other first-aid items. We had maps, compasses, whistles, a wilderness permit filed with the Department of Agriculture, a small fishing rod, a lightweight camera, and other presumed necessities.

The heavy weights of our packs prompted a long discussion aimed at eliminating the unnecessary items. After about an hour of arguing we could only agree on removing one paperback book, with the promise that we would share two others. Not one of us was willing to jettison anything prior to a 15-day trip into the unknown, remote wilderness. After all, you never know what you might need!

John Lazzeri, the hiker who limits himself to 40-pound packs and stays out for months at a time, has an admirable philosophy. He believes that many of us are insecure and that we surround ourselves with possessions to bolster our feelings of self-worth. He and many of his colleagues in the Appalachain Mountain Club and the Appalachain Trail Conference have adopted an unwritten rule. If they hike two weeks without using a particular item they send that item home or discard it, not including medicines. Interestingly this idea often stays with them when they complete their trip and return home. If they don't use an item of clothing within a couple of weeks, they give it to charity.

I know people who think they need a different outfit for every event they attend, buy one, and then complain about lack of closet space and how much things cost nowadays. Conspicuous consumption, or flaunting one's possessions to show off is, as far as I'm concerned, an obvious sign of insecurity and gets in the way of more important values. I don't subscribe to the idea that "clothes make the man". Getting rid of clutter and simplifying life appeals to me. This idea was espoused by Henry David Thoreau, who besides being a writer and a philosopher, was an avid hiker.

By 11:00 a.m. Tomoko had dropped off their children with neighbors and written and signed medical release forms. I purchased a small notebook for diary writing, which turned out to be a prescient move, and Jon bought a "really fine" sheath knife. The moment of our departure had finally arrived. Yosemite, here we come!

Part 2
Lost

"The backpacks were so unwieldy and heavy that we didn't
take them off during the breaks."

Four

Tomoko, Jon and I continually chose Yosemite for our vacations, not so much because it was in California but because it offered us climbing and camping country as rugged and beautiful as anything available in the United States. We could test ourselves against the forces of nature while admiring the continually unfolding majestic creations of a supernatural force we couldn't comprehend. Being in the isolated areas of Yosemite was like being with God and totally away from everyday human materialism.

We never stopped appreciating that such an area had been set aside for us.

The process of creating a national park started on June 30, 1864, when President Abraham Lincoln signed the Yosemite Park Act, setting aside only 60 square miles of land for "public use, resort, and recreation". This area surrounded Yosemite Valley, that seven-mile-long by one-mile-wide stretch that is so popular today. This was the first time in America that the government had done anything to preserve land from development. It led to the establishment of all the other national parks. On October 1, 1890, Yosemite National Park was actually designated and was about 25 times larger than the original area set aside by Lincoln.

Since then there has been an incredible amount of tension and political maneuvering between environmentalists and people who want the park opened for more use and more business exploitation. As the battle continues to rage, the size of the park changes as one group or another has its way. Five hundred forty two square miles were lost in 1905 and the incomparably beautiful Hetch Hetchy Valley was ceded to the city of San Francisco in 1913 for its water supply. There is an ongoing debate about how the citizens of the United States want their national parks managed and protected.

We drove north from Los Angeles, stopping at Groveland, where we checked in with the park rangers, discussed our route and proposed itinerary, and reviewed our wilderness permit. We inquired about the water level of creeks, (some were low, some dried up). The rangers warned us that because of the severe drought we could not count on the springs and streams shown on our maps to be flowing when we reached them. We were advised to fill our canteens and water bags at every opportunity. This turned out to be sage advice and we quickly got into the habit of conserving water. They also warned us of a plethora of black bears in the area we were planning on visiting. We got a crash course on disposing of our garbage.

The rangers were right on target with their warnings of the shortage of water and the abundance of bears and we did our best to comply with their suggestions but, it turned out, we couldn't do enough on either front.

Our next stop was Cherry Lake, a beautiful tree-lined body of water near the northwest corner of the park. We parked our car at the dam, hoping it would be safe for two weeks. Considering the possibility that we might be separated on the trail and that one of us might be required to return to the vehicle, we devised an ingenious hiding place for an extra set of car keys, near to but not in the car.

It didn't take a college professor to notice that the level of the lake was very low. There was a wide ring of bleached rocks and sand forming a white border around the water. We took too much time making final adjustments to our packs, donning an extra pair of socks and putting on our boots. The packs were so heavy that we had to help each other lift them to our backs. We finally started across the dam at 5:45 p.m.

We had problems right away.

The route was extremely difficult, much more so than we had anticipated from the map, and our packs were very heavy. It would have been an effort to walk on flat, smooth ground at sea level. This, however, was nowhere near flat and smooth and we were almost a mile high. The winding trail went steeply uphill and was covered with fallen branches and rocks and boulders deposited by ancient glaciers. The packs themselves represented 30 percent of Jon's and my body weight and 40 percent of Tomoko's. She felt it the most, and we were forced to take frequent breaks. I'm ashamed to admit this but despite my zest for the outdoors and my constant pursuit of physical fitness, I was a cigarette smoker. After all the huffing and puffing up the side of the lake, basically gasping for oxygen, the first thing I did when we rested was light up. It doesn't make any sense to me now. I gave up the habit years ago. The backpacks were so unwieldy and heavy that we didn't take them off during the breaks. We just looked for rock shelves or fallen trees we could back up to and lean on.

After twenty minutes of actual hiking and two

breaks we arrived at our first destination, what should have been a flowing stream. It wasn't flowing and it wasn't a stream. A thin trickle was working its way down the hill. We eagerly gulped cup after cup of cool, clear water and saturated our bandanas and applied them to our faces and necks. It was wonderfully refreshing. We filled our two water bottles, two one-quart bota bags, and the two-quart canteen. The wet aluminum canteen slipped out of Jon's hands, hit a rock, and punctured. Within the first hour of our trip we had lost 25 percent of our water carrying capacity. The warnings of the Groveland park rangers to conserve water resonated in our ears.

By 7:15 we had all had it. It had been an hour and a half of lugging that overwhelming weight up a long ridge overlooking Cherry Lake on a day when the temperature had been in the 90's.

We looked for an area relatively free of rocks and brambles, cleared out the brush, and created our first campsite about 30 yards off the trail.

There are 17 established campgrounds spread around the park. They range from rather primitive to very comfortable. Some provide features such as running water, flush toilets, fire pits, picnic table/bench combinations, telephones, park rangers for control, safety, and information, garbage cans, and cleared spaces for tents. We eschewed all of those comforts for our trip and we were proud of our independence and self-sufficiency. The campgrounds probably don't enhance the beauty of the park but they surely facilitate more people enjoying it.

After pitching my tent, we checked our lists so that we knew which pack to open for Tuesday's dinner. Because of the drought we were very careful building a fire and cooked a most welcome freeze-dried meal.

After dinner we were sitting around the dying campfire enjoying a cognac when suddenly we heard voices and the sounds of horses approaching. Our reactions ranged from fear to terror. We felt extremely vulnerable sitting together in the glow of the fire, completely isolated and without weapons of any kind. We became silent and motionless. The movie *Deliverance* came to mind. The riders and their mounts continued up the trail either ignoring us or not noticing the fire through the trees.

This incident prompted a heated discussion that evening, much of which involved the fact that if anything happened to all three of us there was no way for any of our friends or family to know about it. Our bodies would remain in a national park until discovered by other hikers or search parties, probably weeks or even months later. This sounds like I've been watching too much television again, but actual events that have been in the news recently make this scenario more plausible.

Many overnight hikers have an unwritten rule of the trail. When you meet someone, be courteous but don't ask questions and don't answer them. Never say you're alone and or divulge your destination. A vague answer to a question about your destination is best, e.g., "I don't really know yet. I might hike a few more miles or more, depending on how I'm feeling." Some hikers deliberately confuse strangers by telling them that they are the vanguard and the rest of the group is about a mile back.

We devised a plan for the future. If we heard people approaching at night, I would go into the woods, hide myself, and watch my friends. Then, it seemed, we would have some options. I might, for example, yell from the darkness that I had a rifle aimed at any intruders, or something like, "Are you folks okay?" as if I was from another group camping nearby. We hoped that this would so surprise and scare the unwelcome visitors that they would quickly leave us and look for some less prepared and more vulnerable hikers. This seems a bit naïve now, but it was the only plan we could come up with.

"...the evergreens were growing in rows formed from cracks in the rock. It looked like one tree was following another from the lake up the ridge."

Five

We rose early Wednesday morning hopeful of making more progress, and enjoying it more, than the day before. Less than wonderful powdered eggs were on the menu. After we had eaten them and cleaned up we made sure that the fire was totally out. By eight o'clock we were back on the trail. Tuesday's hike had been difficult, but this was impossible. We were headed toward Kibbe Lake, seven miles away. It became a forced seven mile march, often ascending steeply, but always ascending. We gained 1,800 feet in elevation from 4,700 feet above sea level at the Cherry Lake dam to 6,500 feet at Kibbe Lake. About an hour into our trek we encountered a group of backpackers coming from the opposite direction.

They couldn't stop talking about unbelievable hordes of malevolent mosquitoes at the lake.

With constant breaks sandwiched between brief periods of hiking, it took us hours to make our way upward through tall incense cedars and ponderosa pines, thick bushes and sometimes open trail. We arrived at a pine grove neatly carpeted with pine needles offering a wonderful fragrance and a welcome respite from the hot sun. It was almost as if a benevolent superior being had placed the grove in our path and put up a sign that said, "eat lunch here". We did eat lunch there and there was, in fact, a sign, but it said "Dead Horse Gulch". Sounded like something out of a Bret Harte novel but don't ask me what it was supposed to signify. The cheese, dried fruit, and candy renewed our energy and the spring water we washed it down with relieved our parched throats. It would have been a wonderful luxury to tarry there a while, taking a nap on the pine needles, but because we were making such slow progress we didn't think we had that option.

When we planned our trip we had thought that we could hike two to three miles an hour. In retrospect that was out of the question even if the ground had been flat, open and at sea level. The weight of the packs and the fact that the weight frequently shifted was making every step difficult. Our energy was being sapped, our hearts were racing, our bodies were dripping sweat. When we took stock of our progress, we found that we were averaging about one mile an hour. We also observed that our breaks were getting longer, our periods of hiking shorter. Of course my cigarette smoking wasn't helping my breathing. When we had laid out the plan on paper at Jon and Tomoko's house, we thought it would be reasonable to hike for 20 minutes and break for five. On the trail we realized that it wasn't possible to plan this way. In actuality our ratio was more like 1:1. We rested the same amount of time that we hiked. What really determined hiking/break times was a combination of our stamina, the terrain, and the elevation gain.

A little past four in the afternoon we, suddenly and without warning, broke out of the woods and were astounded by an incredible sight. Kibbe Lake was breathtakingly gorgeous. It literally stopped us in our tracks. We couldn't do anything but stare. It was so clear, so smooth, so quiet, so blue, so primitive. It would have been easy to convince ourselves that we were explorers who had just discovered something that no human had ever seen. The trees came right down to the water's edge. They were formidable, straight and imposing. It was obvious that they had been around a long time. They were reflected all around the glassy surface of the lake. The reflections were so clear and detailed that either the trees or their images could have been the reality. The lake was surrounded by irregular shaped granite and the evergreens were growing in rows formed from cracks in the rock. It looked like one tree was following another from the lake up the ridge. At the north end of Kibbe were two immense granite monoliths with rounded tops. Were they gods placed there to overlook and protect us?

As our elevation had increased, I noticed that the flowers and trees around us were changing. Here at Kibbe Lake there were no deciduous trees in sight.

Once long ago I had to drive from southern Maine to Washington, D.C., in one day. When I left early on an autumn morning, I noticed that the trees were bald, leaves dead on the ground. As I passed though a succession of states I marveled that leaves were still on the trees and that the colors were changing the further south I drove. In Maine there was virtually no color, then yellow leaves started appearing, and gradually as I drove on, the leaves turned to shades of orange and then red. The variety of vegetation also changed. Yosemite, in a much smaller geographic area, is a wonderful example of this phenomenon.

In a very compact area, five life zones, or continental regions are evident. You can tell which one you're in by the vegetation that's present, although it's not infallible because some plants grow in more than one zone. Another interesting aspect is that you can be on the same mountain, at the same elevation, and have totally different vegetation depending on which way the slope faces.

Vegetation growth varies with sun and wind exposure, amount of precipitation, and the consistency and composition of the soil. Trees and plants facing south get more sunlight so grow taller. Trees blasted by high winds at higher elevations can't grow as high.

We started our trip in the lowest zone, the Upper Sonoran. It's really the foothills and ranges from 500 feet up to about 1500. There is little snow and it doesn't rain from April to November so the ground is dry. We couldn't count on intermittent streams being there for us. The digger pine is the most prevalent tree but there are also live oaks and sycamores. The live oak is unique in that it keeps its leaves year round. Flowers bloom in March but are gone by May.

We spent most of our two weeks in the next zone up, the Transition Zone. On western exposures it starts at 1,200 feet and on southern slopes it rises to 9,000 feet. Here the 200 feet high yellow pine, or ponderosa, is the dominant tree. There are also plenty of white firs. We were looking at both varieties at Kibbe Lake. The mountain misery, a delicate looking five petal flower native to this zone, was valued by the Miwok Indians. They used its pungent leaves to make a tea which they thought to be a panacea.

After admiring Kibbe Lake's incomparable scenery, our thoughts turned to more pragmatic issues. We had not seen anyone in six hours and assumed that we were alone. There was only one thing to do—strip off our clothes and let the cool, clean water revive us. We desperately needed to wash away the dirt, grime and sweat that had accumulated on our bodies over the past two days. The air was still hot and dry. Never had a body of water looked so inviting.

The three of us had been naked together before. We had visited nude beaches on many occasions and had hiked and camped for extended periods in various places around the United States. This, however, was the first time that the situation had come up in an unfamiliar setting since Jon had asked me to be a sex surrogate. To say I was uneasy would be a gross understatement. Tomoko took the lead by dropping her pack on the sandy beach, taking off her shirts and bra and then her jeans and panties. I figured that I should follow her lead and quickly removed my clothes. Jon did the same.

While looking at Tomoko, a feeling of tenderness came over me. She looked so small, innocent and vulnerable. I wanted to protect her but I didn't understand from what. I was also surprised to be sensing some sexual arousal in myself and strode briskly into the lake to hide any potential problems. As I passed her I thought I saw her give me a meaningful stare but there was no way that I could interpret it under these circumstances. Soon we were all in the lake shouting to each other how wonderful the chilly water felt and how amazing it was to be there. The lake was deep blue, the trees a dark green, the mountains slate gray, and the sky was dotted with bright sunlit white clouds creating a stark contrast with the azure blue sky. My anxiety and any sexual feelings were literally dampened and cooled off by Kibbe Lake.

Being in such a pristine environment was an incredible experience, and all three of us wallowed in it. I swim laps as a regular activity but in the local high school pool I must wear a bathing suit, "Proper swimming attire is mandatory." When packing for this trip we never anticipated a need for swim suits. It's such a luxurious, sensual feeling having cool water pass directly over my body. I couldn't get enough of this refreshing break to our otherwise difficult day. The 360 degree vista visible from the center of the lake is something I will never forget.

The setting was so beautiful and we were so tired that it didn't take long to decide to camp by the lake. In retrospect we should have moved back into the woods and hiked a bit longer. None of us had ever experienced anything like what happened when darkness settled over us.

On public television nature programs, I've often heard narrators talk about flocks of birds darkening the sky. Our sky was darkened, but not by birds. Hordes, armies, societies, I don't know how to describe them, but it seemed like every mosquito in the Western World had heard the chief mosquito send out an urgent message summoning all available volunteers to Kibbe Lake in California.

It was absolutely amazing. During our swim we never noticed an insect and we were nude. Now, fully clothed to protect us from the evening chill, we were attacked from every direction. The mass whining itself was unnerving. The combined effect of seeing, hearing and feeling the clouds of mosquitoes drove us into feverish activity. Nothing mattered except to get away from the swarms of unrelenting, biting aggressors. The three of us raced to pitch my two man pup tent, trying to protect ourselves as we worked. As soon as it was up we entered, scrunched up so we all fit, zipped the entrance and spent the whole night listening to thousands of mosquitoes trying to get to us. We saw their silhouettes on the outside of the sheer, orange nylon tent. They were so thick it appeared that the fabric was printed instead of solid. The noise was so unsettling and the conditions so crowded that we could only take short naps.

Our stress and fatigue from that day and night might help to explain our behavior in the next days.

Just as quickly as they had come, they were gone. I once was in a biology class at Cornell University when my professor said that in the ecological system of the planet every creature had a reason for being and was involved in a relationship with every other living thing. I raised my hand and asked what purpose mosquitoes served. After thinking briefly he responded that they were food for birds and bats. I looked at him to see if he was serious. He was. I can't imagine a single bird that would die of starvation if mosquitoes became extinct.

If I were in charge, I would increase the number of mosquito-eating birds and bats to make mosquitoes extinct. Bats actually eat more mosquitoes than do birds. But I'm not in charge nor am I an ornithologist. Another mystery to me is: Where are all the male mosquitoes? I'm told that only the females bite and I have the distinct impression that they all bite so they must all be female. The argument that females need the protein in human blood to nurture their eggs does not garner any sympathy from me, nor does it make me a more willing donor. Incidentally, the scientific answer to my rhetorical question, where are all the males, is that they are off drinking nectar someplace. How nice.

Thursday morning when I exited the tent, the

sun was just beginning to appear above the tree tops. There was no sign of the mosquitoes. A section of the eastern sky had turned mellow shades of mauve, pink, and orange. Jon and Tomoko were soon up and about and we cooked a wonderful breakfast of pancakes and apple butter. We ate it on the beach in order to, once again, appreciate the beauty of Kibbe Lake. After cleaning up we gathered the clothes that we had so impulsively strewn all over the beach the previous evening when we had gone for a swim. While the breakfast fire was still alive we boiled some lake water and filled the bota bags. By the time we had air dried the dew-laden sleeping gear and doused the fire it was 9:10 when we rejoined the trail.

At one of our morning breaks, Jon told us of his new idea, that he had spotted a possible "shortcut" on the map. At this point, only two days out, we would do anything to shorten the hiking and backpack carrying distance. We eagerly looked over his shoulder as his finger traced a cross-country route to the top of a ridgeline. The trail we were following eventually wound its way to this ridgeline but we could cut out all the meanderings, and about three miles, by taking a direct line and then picking it up at the summit. After all, the shortest distance between two points... . When Jon finished his explanation, Tomoko and I jumped at the idea.

This was easily the worst decision we made on

the whole trip and led to our worst experience. Geological Survey maps we were using were at a scale of 1:25,000. That means one centimeter on the map represents 250 meters on the ground. This intense scale is like a magnifying glass. Virtually every feature on the ground is visible. Structures such as water towers, schools, and churches are named. Elevation is shown by contour lines, each of which is six meters from the next. To show steepness, the contour lines are bunched. The farther away the contour lines are from each other, the more gradual the climb and the elevation gain. Mountains with vegetation are shown in green, those that are bald, usually at the peaks, are depicted in white. Water features are clearly delineated in blue. We had a lot of information at our disposal and we thought we were using it efficiently during our planning process. Another one of our misjudgments.

"Avoiding three miles of trail represented saving three hours of hot, step-by-step dragging of our weary bodies, pressed down by the infernal 55-pound weights attached to our backs."

Six

If Yogi Berra said, "If there's a fork in the road, take it," then I would like to paraphrase, "If you have a chance to stay on a trail with or without a fork, do it." Any experienced hiker could have told us that in this wild country so far away from any other humans we should have opted to be as safe as possible. You have to empathize with our sorry plight to be able to understand why we made such a stupid decision. We were so hot, so tired and so discouraged, that any possibility of carrying our packs and ourselves over a shorter distance sounded wonderful. Avoiding three miles of trail represented saving three hours of hot, step-by-step dragging of our weary bodies, pressed down by the infernal 55-pound weights attached to our backs.

The idea sounded so simple. We would hike cross-country, up the mountain, and meet our trail where it joined and followed the ridge line. We had a compass so we would be able to shoot an azimuth and follow a precise line to the ridge. Even if we met the ridge at an unplanned location it wouldn't matter because the trail followed the ridge and we had to intersect it sooner or later. The logic was clear. If there's a long river somewhere ahead of you, you know that if you keep heading in its direction that eventually you'll intersect with it. We also identified an intermittent creek on the map so this short cut could expedite replenishing our water supplies.

The decision was easy to make and unanimous. We were proud of ourselves for having found the new route and the idea of saving time and miles rejuvenated our sagging spirits.

It took three hours to reach the ridge, the same time we had allocated for the trail. But the route to the ridge turned out to be unbelievably difficult. There was no evidence that any human had ever traversed this area.

Thousands of years ago glaciers had pushed huge boulders along, depositing them at random on their relentless flow west. When the ice age ended, the glaciers melted and retreated but the boulders stayed in place—directly in our way. We had to either march around or over them. If we elected to go over them we had to help each other up and try to lift the packs separately. A further complication was the fact that thick, thorny bushes had grown around and over the rocks forming something like a barbed wire barrier.

And finally we had to deal with the air force. The mosquitoes were back—or rather, we had invaded their home base. There was little tree cover, so no shade. The sun was unmerciful and the swarming hordes of buzzing, biting mosquitoes seemed to renew their energy as they landed on every exposed part of our bodies and packs. The noise in our ears was deafening. The hiking was so enervating that we just had to stop to catch our breath from time to time. That was when the opportunistic mosquitoes landed on us en masse. We were totally carpeted with them. Our packs were covered. We couldn't believe how many mosquitoes there were and what mean and aggressive dispositions they had. The bites on our faces, necks, and hands were itching terribly but we were so busy using our arms and hands to wave the attackers away that we had no time to scratch.

There was nothing to do but continue the climb, negotiating the obstacles on the ground and in the air the best we could. We tried to limit our break time so that we could get past the open, treeless areas as fast as possible.

Squinting through sweat burned eyes, we finally achieved the ridge line thinking that our immediate problems were over. We fully expected to see the trail. Our expectations were quickly dashed. We couldn't find a trail anywhere. On the map there was a very obvious line of little dashes working their way over and around the contour lines and winding onto the ridge. This line was so evident that it never occurred to us that, on the ground, the trail might be obscured by rocks or vegetation. As far as I know now, trails in such remote areas were not maintained on a regular basis. For upkeep they were dependent on frequent use by hikers and their boots. We looked in all directions but there wasn't a clue. The trail we were following was not blazed on trees, only showing on the ground, and through years of disuse, had virtually disappeared in many places. We were actually looking for something that might no longer exist. This added to our frustration and discouragement.

Time to become more efficient. Time for a plan. We dropped our bright orange packs under one of the larger trees and pulled out our whistles. Jon thought the trail should be a bit north of where we were. Tomoko opined that it was probably in the gully 500 yards south, and I didn't have the slightest inclination. We each headed off in different directions vowing to return to the tree in 30 minutes with a report. We also agreed to blow our whistles periodically so that we would keep within hearing distance of each other. As Tomoko left us she muttered that cross-country hiking was "psychologically depressing." Tomoko had had a particularly difficult time climbing the mountain as her small frame had to support a very heavy backpack over terribly difficult terrain. I think that the physical exhaustion coupled with the frustration of not finding the trail was largely responsible for her growing emotional deterioration.

Jon and I, being men and therefore much stronger emotionally (ha!), didn't say anything. I actually thought that Jon was in a lot worse shape than his wife. During the grueling climb up the mountain his tone had changed from conversational and logical to whining and irrational. He kept second guessing himself for planning the cross-country route and wondered aloud if any of us would get out of this alive. I thought that this was a bit extreme but when there are only three of you, alone in such a harsh environment and mutually dependent, sensible people don't use the opportunity to chastise or criticize. Being sensible, I didn't say anything to Jon, but his increasingly despondent exclamations had me worried.

Had I been alone I never would have opted for a cross-country route. It would have been better to be safe than sorry, but since there were three of us I think we felt that we could take care of one another. We should have factored in that we were inexperienced hikers and were emotionally and physically exhausted. Like so many people, we had reached for immediate gratification at the expense of measured thinking and were now paying the price.

I headed back to the tree 30 minutes after we separated. Jon was already there. Tomoko wasn't. Jon and I compared notes only to find that neither of us had found any positive signs of a trail. We continued to wait for Tomoko. We had started our search a little after noon, now it was approaching one o'clock. All of a sudden Jon yelled, "TOMOKO!" Coming unexpectedly, it scared the hell out of me. There was no response. Jon had even intimidated the birds. We were listening to total silence.

In an effort to do something that seemed constructive and to try to make Jon feel better, I started yelling Tomoko's name too. We soon adopted a policy of alternatively yelling and blowing our whistles. After each initiative we waited, hoping to hear a response. Nothing. Next we started to venture away from the tree, in opposite directions, continuing to yell and blow. We searched an ever increasing radius from the tree making sure to keep in ear-shot of each other. Slow-moving minutes turned into an hour. At this point I think we were both coming to the realization that we weren't going to find her this way, but neither wanted to give voice to his conclusion.

If Tomoko was still in the area she either couldn't hear us or could hear but wasn't able to respond. Both of these alternatives were ominous. The logical conclusion would be that she was unconscious, paralyzed, or dead. Yosemite has poisonous snakes and dangerous animals. The terrain itself was hazardous. A fall into a crevice or down a steep slope was well within the realm of possibility. Tomoko was exhausted from the high altitude cross-country climb and she was extremely despondent. If hypothermia set in, it could affect her ability to think clearly and make sound decisions under stress. There were a myriad of factors that might have done her in.

Another possibility was that she had ventured beyond the immediate area and was perfectly fine. In this scenario she had to be lost or she would have returned to the tree where our packs lay.

I became lost twice looking for her because of the thick trees and brush. No matter where I was, everything looked the same. It was confusing walking through dense groves of similar looking pine trees looking for just the one tree with our packs under it. I had two panic attacks thinking that I was lost but worked my way out of my muddle each time. Fortunately our packs were bright orange and virtually glowed in the shady grove.

For the first time in my life I found myself

cursing trees. Why did they have to be so big, grow in such dense groves and all look the same?

The trees in Yosemite are actually amazing. Included in the first 60 square miles of the park was the Mariposa Grove of giant sequoias. It covered 250 acres with more than 500 redwood trees. Known also as *Sequoiadendron giganteum* and "the big trees" by the native Indians, these are the oldest living things on the planet. They sometimes reach heights of 300 feet. When they grow beyond 200 feet they are vulnerable to lightning strikes and their tops are sheared off. Many of the standing trees are 200 feet tall. The bark on the larger trees ranges from six inches to two feet thick. The largest tree still standing has been named Grizzly Giant for easy reference. It is 209 feet tall, 32 feet in diameter, and has a volume of 30,000 cubic feet with limbs as thick as ten feet. It is estimated to be between 2,700 and 3,800 years old. Sequoias don't die of old age. They succumb to the weight and pressure of glaciers or to the logger's saw. One large sequoia can yield as much lumber as a one-acre pine forest. This is a big temptation to loggers and brings them into conflict with environmentalists.

Sequoias reproduce from minute seeds enclosed in tiny pine cones. An average tree produces 200 seed-bearing cones. It takes about 91,000 seeds to weigh just one pound. The seeds escape the cones when insects, animals, birds or fire create holes in the cone. It seems strange, but fire, which one thinks of as an enemy to trees, actually facilitates new growth. The fires in the 1980s sparked much debate about proper forest management. Some seeds cannot set in the ground if they fall on forest litter. Fire clears out the ground debris making it possible for the next generation of trees to propagate. Bears also can benefit from forest fires by using hollowed out tree trunks for their winter dens. These forests had been growing through many thousands of years of lightning strikes before human fire fighters came along, and they seem to have survived quite well. The debate about whether or not to fight forest fires continues.

As I kept searching for Tomoko, all I saw were trees. They blocked my long range vision and created an atmosphere that pushed me to the brink of claustrophobia.

In our mental and physical state and in this location it was easy to imagine an entire panoply of possibilities for Tomoko. I remembered that she was dressed in a skimpy tank top and had no sweater. That was hardly protection against the cool evenings and cold nights. If we couldn't find her by evening, the probability of hypothermia had to be taken seriously. In her condition, hypothermia could easily be fatal. Then I realized that she had not even taken any water with her, probably thinking she'd be back at her pack within minutes. The more I thought about the situation, the more anxious I became.

It was time for Jon and me to deal with the issue up front and figure out what to do. We sat under the tree and started assessing our situation. Jon immediately began sobbing uncontrollably. The previous night's sleep deprivation due to the mosquitoes, the morning's hike up the mountain, the search for Tomoko, and the mental and emotional anxiety had obviously gotten to him. It's hard, at this point, for me to be critical. It was his wife that was lost, not mine, and each of us brings different emotional and mental strengths and weaknesses to any given situation. What was clear to me was that I had been thrust, unwillingly and unintentionally, into a position where I had to be strong. I had to provide calmness, unflappability, common sense, and logic to my emotionally exhausted friend.

I was ready to assume this role but before I had a chance I became really upset. Jon started whining about what his life would be like if we never found Tomoko or if we found her dead. How would he be able to go to work on time everyday and still take care of his children? Who would take care of his day-to-day chores? How was he supposed to do research and publish while shopping for food and cooking for four people? He envisioned the unraveling of his economically efficient marriage model, and he didn't like it. It had taken him a long time to develop his ideal marriage arrangement, and now in one short unexpected episode on a supposedly benign hiking trip, it was all coming apart.

Listening to Jon whimper his concerns I felt myself getting angrier by the minute. I could feel my cheeks flushing, my teeth clenching, and my hands tightening into fists. He sounded cold, unsympathetic and incredibly self-centered. I suddenly saw a spoiled brat in a man's body thinking only of himself. I had to get up and walk away to control myself. On the one hand my friend had lost his wife and was in a terrible emotional state and I had sympathy. On the other, this self-confident, professorial prig was demonstrating the most selfish and insensitive behavior I had ever witnessed. I couldn't believe I was hearing this drivel. I wanted to reach out and slap him. I wanted to yell at him to shut up.

My reaction to the incident had been totally different. Feeling empathy for Tomoko, I was hoping she wasn't hurt, suffering, or feeling the frustration and fear of being lost in such a forbidding locale. I was thinking of her children who might lose their mother, the one parent who really cared for them and was responsible for the maintenance of their daily existence. I was thinking about people close to Tomoko, her parents, her friends, me, who might be losing someone very important in our lives.

Tomoko had once commented to me about feeling that Jon only appreciated what she did, not who she was. Jon didn't give a damn about her, he was only using her to satisfy his own needs and this moment brought that out in spades. Fortunately, no matter what happened, Tomoko would never have to learn how selfishly Jon had reacted.

I just couldn't imagine all the possible scenarios for Tomoko, but I thought that the very fact that she had not returned to our tree presaged a bad ending.

Seven

I yelled at Jon to stop complaining, that it wasn't accomplishing anything and that we had to do something constructive before we lost our daylight. He agreed and we proceeded to develop a plan. There seemed to be nothing more that we could do there so we decided that the best thing we could do was to go for help. Those woods were too expansive, too dense, and too dangerous for us to try to find Tomoko by ourselves. We would only increase the possibility of our getting lost or injured. So the idea we developed was that Jon would take a minimum amount of food and water and try to run back to the Cherry Lake Dam and our car. Since it was about two o'clock and the route was all downhill, we thought that by traveling light he might make it by dark.

His proposed route would intersect Kibbe Lake so he could fill his canteen there rather than depleting our meager existing stock of water. I would remain and pitch my tent. After much discussion of alternatives we decided that if I didn't hear from him after three full days, I would take the same route back, taking as much equipment as was reasonably comfortable to carry and leave the rest. It seemed very important to both of us that one of us should stay in the area to continue a search for Tomoko or to be there in case she was able to find her way back to the tree.

Our hope was that Jon would somehow be able to enlist the help of some kind of a search party. We thought of rangers on horseback, a mule train, and helicopters. All had been used in Yosemite rescues in the past. I would simply stay and leave my neon orange tent exposed in an open site that would be visible from the air.

At that time it didn't occur to me to think about what I would do in this rugged, potentially dangerous area, by myself, for three days. I was only glad to be planning a constructive course of action. I had become obsessed with Tomoko's plight.

Jon left for Cherry Lake at 3:10. I watched him as long as I could as he disappeared into the trees down the hill. I wondered if I would ever see him, or Tomoko, again. His emotional state was frazzled like no one's I had ever seen.

Immediately I was aware of being alone. Totally alone. I was isolated from human help or companionship of any kind. It scared the hell out of me. Suddenly I was invaded by panic and terror. All kinds of worst case scenarios began pushing themselves into my mind. What if my appendix burst or I was attacked by coyotes or mountain lions? What would I do if a rattlesnake bit me? Needing to do something to take my mind off these macabre thoughts, I undid the three packs and started to take a mental inventory of each. I sorted the food so that I would have it handy for my meals and snacks and thought about what would make a good dinner for that night.

Suddenly I remembered Tomoko. I yelled her name as loud as I could and blew my whistle. I listened for a response. Nothing. I decided to repeat this routine every 15 minutes, hoping too that it might scare off any animals. I wondered where, and how, Jon was, imagining that after an hour and a half he had found Kibbe Lake, replenished his water, taken a brief rest, and continued on.

Thinking about Tomoko and Jon kept my

mind off my own rather bleak situation. Organizing my food diverted me from the potential dangers around me. I had to keep busy, mentally and physically, or the terror would return. I wondered, if Jon was able to reach the car, would it start? If he could find the ranger station, would it be open at that hour? In my growing insecurity I was gradually beginning to lose my composure. I wondered if Tomoko was lying hurt and conscious and helpless somewhere, perhaps dying of thirst and hypothermia. I blew my whistle. It shattered the stillness and my consciousness.

My thoughts turned to self-preservation. I required protection from the night and I needed to pitch my tent. I found an open spot on the ridge line with an incredible view of an enormous valley. The tops of the mountains in the distance were jagged and irregular and covered with snow. It was easy to understand why they had been named the Sierra Nevada. In Spanish, *Sierra* means sawtooth and *Nevada* is snow covered. I marveled at nature's grandeur and how lucky I was to be a part of it.

It is generally believed that the Sierra Nevada was formed between ten and 80 million years ago when an enormous, geological uplift pushed layers of granite lying under the ocean up into a formidable mountain range. The range is 400 miles long and is still rising. Cracks and crevices in the rocks gave erosive forces a chance to carve canyons. During the ice ages at least three glaciers did their part to enlarge the canyons, up to 3,000 feet deep, and create valleys. Two of them, the Merced and Tenaya glaciers, merged near Half Dome and carved out Yosemite Valley. They continued to El Portal, 15 miles to the west. Ten thousand to 15,000 years ago the last glacier retreated, leaving many waterfalls and more than 200 lakes. The mountains are over 8,000 feet high. Mt. Whitney, the highest in the Sierra Nevada, and in the 48 original states, reaches up 14,495 feet. The upper, middle, and lower Yosemite Falls total more than 2,400 feet.

Yosemite could boast (if a national park could talk) of having the highest waterfall in North America, three of the world's ten tallest waterfalls, the tallest and largest single granite monolith in the world (El Capitan) and one of the world's largest trees. The Merced and Tuolumne Rivers had done their part in adding to the exquisite scenery by carving out valleys and leaving lakes as they meandered through the countryside. There is truly an amazing amount of natural features in such a limited space!

Standing on layers of pure granite, I was finding it difficult to locate dirt deep enough to pound my tent pegs into. Moving away from the edge a bit I found a spot where the tent would be visible from the air and also a little protected from the wind. After the tent was secure, I blew the whistle over the valley. I imagined it could be heard for a hundred miles and that no one was there to hear it. I felt like I was the last human on earth.

I ventured back to the packs and rummaged through the plastic bags of food. I immediately noticed how quiet it was. The only sounds were the wind blowing through the trees, the buzzing of flies and that awful whining of mosquitoes. From time to time I heard the mocking chatter of birds. (Was I getting paranoid, thinking the birds were mocking me?) From the base of the tree I could see ants, large, reddish ants, crawling up and over everything. They seemed to be searching for something at random and yet there was an organization about their foraging. Flies were setting on me constantly but I was at a point where I only brushed away the mosquitoes. I was convinced that I, the human being, was the center of attention of all living things in the immediate area.

There were lots of deer around. Jon and I had come upon one earlier in the day and I had seen several more in my search for Tomoko. They didn't run when they saw me. I imagined that they had never before seen a human and didn't know to be afraid. Rather, they stood their ground and stared at me without moving. I stared back, marveling at how gentle and innocent they appeared. They seemed to be able to rotate their heads 180 degrees without moving another muscle. Eventually the deer became bored with me and moved away, intent on munching on the bushes. The deer helped to calm me. They made the environment seem more gentle, less threatening.

I decided I could reduce the duration of my anxiety by limiting my periods of wakefulness. Therefore, scheduling an early dinner and bedtime seemed the thing to do. I still had a few fresh carrots and I supplemented these with a cold, freeze-dried meal. That isolated, arid, breezy country was not the place for me to build a fire. As I was eating, a woodpecker added a percussion section to the violin-like whirring of the mosquitoes. It was amazing how I literally tuned into the sounds around me. Usually I'm oblivious to the sounds of nature.

I could feel the chill settling about me, so I added a warm sweater to my daytime outfit. The breeze picked up as the sun offered me less and less warmth and cast a weaker light and longer shadows. My apprehension grew with the increasing chill and deepening darkness.

I fantasized that Tomoko had fallen and hit her head and that this cooler air would revive her. I half expected her to appear, walking up the mountain toward me. In my vision, she had a sheepish grin as if to say, "Can you believe that I did something so stupid?" But she didn't appear, and I had to direct my mind to a different train of thought.

I thought about my surroundings. This was such a remote place, nine miles from the dam and another ten to a village. I was about 7,000 feet up, almost to the snow line. All around me were huge uplifted mountains, ridges of hard, bald, unyielding granite and tall, straight pines.

I had never been so far away from civilization. I had always coveted quiet and natural beauty around me. Now that I had it, I hated it.

Time for bed and I snuggled into my sleeping bag, making very, very sure that my sheer tent was thoroughly zipped closed. I lay there listening to the sounds around me. My thoughts immediately turned to Tomoko and Jon. I felt so frustrated that I didn't know where Tomoko was and in what condition. I so much wanted to help her and couldn't. The only thing I could think of doing was to blow my stupid whistle. Nothing but the flies and mosquitoes answered its shrill blast. Nothing. I relived the afternoon in my mind, how I had returned to the top of the hill to the point where Tomoko had disappeared. I had blown my whistle and called her name. I had yelled at the trees. Trees usually seem so pretty but today they didn't. They seemed stately, ominous, impenetrable, concealing.

I fell asleep quickly. It had been one of the most stressful and emotionally and physically daunting days of my life. During the night I thought I heard animals breathing and walking near my tent. I was so tired that I didn't bother to rouse myself from my groggy stupor.

Bright sunlight shining on my face awakened me. I lay in my sleeping bag listening. It was quiet. I got up, unzipped the tent and walked around. There were a number of signs that I had been visited by nocturnal animals. The stools, or skat, as outdoor people euphemistically refer to them, seemed to be from a bear. There also were deer droppings but I was familiar with them. They looked like small, round, solid black pebbles. What I was looking at was much more imposing. Whatever species had made this contribution to my campsite had my utmost respect and I hoped it would not choose to make a daytime appearance.

The day turned out to be pretty routine. Breakfast, lunch, and dinner were sandwiched around short forays around the area yelling, "TOMOKO," and blowing the whistle. During the day the flies were ubiquitous, the mosquitoes absent. (They were probably attending strategy meetings about how to attack me from all directions, make maximum disconcerting noise near my ears, and bite any exposed fleshy areas. But wherever they were, I was grateful that they weren't around me.)

I tried to keep myself busy by reading one of the paperbacks in Jon's pack, but it's not easy to concentrate on a novel when you're continually swatting at flies. After giving up on the book, I had plenty of time for reflection. Intensely aware of the beauty around me and feeling overwhelmed by the heights of the trees and mountains, I marveled at how small man is upon the earth and how much we delude ourselves about our imagined self-importance. At the same time I had a strong feeling of being a part of the world. It was a mystical feeling of oneness with the total universe. I tried to answer for myself the unanswerable; why are we here, what are we supposed to do, if indeed we are supposed to do anything? Is there a creator of all this grandeur and purpose in nature or is it simply to be explained by scientific principles? Why are there rocks and trees and deer and ants and people? Is there a beginning, and if so, how and why? If comets came together in a big explosion, where did the comets come from and what was there before them?

Prolonged thinking of such subjects could have given me a headache, so I turned to more prosaic thoughts, ones that I might be able to answer. If Tomoko was dead, what were my obligations toward Jon? How did I feel about Jon after observing his sniveling and egotistic reactions? Would our relationship ever be the same? If Tomoko was all right, what happened to her? Would I have to come down from this mountain myself or would I be rescued?

Between whistle blowing, name yelling, eating, reading, and thinking, the day moved along quickly. Mindful of the previous night's visitors I decided to separate all the food from the three packs and string it up between two trees. The park rangers had told us that this could prevent bears from feasting on our provisions. I did the best I could with what I had. I selected a sturdy tree far from my tent site. I tied the end of a rope to a rock, then tied the food packet to the rope about ten feet away from the rock. Using the rock as a weight, I threw the rope over the far end of an overhanging limb, and pulled the rope until the food was elevated. Finally I looped the rope around the tree trunk. The food was swinging about ten feet off the ground and about the same distance from the trunk.

I watched the sun sink over the granite cliffs at 8:40, and five minutes later it was dark. I couldn't believe how many stars I could see and how bright they were.

If you don't mind feeling small, find yourself a perch 7,000 feet above electric lights, and just look around you in all directions. The phrase "awe inspiring" could have been created in such a setting.

After getting a good fix of my universe and starting to shiver from the ever-increasing cold, I retreated to my tent. Blessed tent, womb in the Sierras. I was finally away from the mosquitoes. I lay in my sleeping bag wondering if tomorrow I would be rescued and learn about Tomoko's fate. I slept fitfully, but I slept.

Eight

Saturday morning dawned bright and cold. I lay in my tent relishing the warmth and security of my sleeping bag. Having now spent two nights on the mountain alone I noticed that I was beginning to adjust to my environment, feeling more in control and less anxious. Noises that had alarmed me two days ago were taken more in stride and I wasn't so jumpy. I enjoyed the chattering birds and tried to pick out individual conversations. The wind was making its presence felt. I watched the sides of the tent alternately blowing in and releasing, and the back and forth flapping of the roof. The wind created a whooshing sound that seemed to start far away and got louder as it came closer, much like an approaching train.

The first thing I did when I was outside the tent was look for the food bag. Relief, it was still there. I had no clue if I had stymied prowling bears, raccoons, and coyotes, or had just been lucky. I resumed my "lonely vigil mode" which meant calling out for Tomoko and blowing my whistle but by this time I had really given up all hope of her showing up. I had pretty well decided that she had somehow figured out how to get back to the car, secured the hidden keys and driven to safety. What was the point of worrying about unseen, hidden dangers?

I noticed that instead of talking to myself I was now talking out loud, even shouting my exclamations. I heard my "SHE'S FINE DAMN IT!" bouncing off the tree trunks and I smiled. This was becoming kind of fun. I have long believed that we bring our own happiness to any situation. Our perceptions make our reality. If I decided to make the best of my circumstances, then everything would be okay. If I chose to worry about every little thing I was sure to drive myself crazy. Chose is the operative word there because I truly believe that we have the ability to choose whether or not we should worry about something. My worrying about Tomoko and Jon wasn't going to change whatever state they were in. I had my own problems and I had decided to deal with them in a very positive way.

I made myself a lemonade for breakfast. I decided that if I prepared and ate one thing at a time it would help the time pass more quickly. If I prepared a whole breakfast, then how would I occupy myself until lunch?

I had searched Tomoko's pack for her whistle and was glad to find that it wasn't there. She had to have it with her. Jon also had his. I was thinking that I should tune my personal antennae for that sound because, if I was going to be rescued, it was more than likely going to be announced by whistle blowing.

When Tomoko had given me a whistle in Los Angeles I had laughed and asked her what it was for. I wasn't laughing now.

The daily parade of the insects had started. New varieties had appeared and they weren't welcome. Red flies and very aggressive bees were all around me. The packs were covered with swarms of flies. The funny thing was that I was enduring all this knowing that I couldn't help Tomoko. She clearly wasn't in the area anymore, but I had promised Jon that I would stay there, so I did.

I started to plan ahead. I decided that if no one came by the next day I would leave early in the morning with a light pack and head for Kibbe Lake. The memory of that clear, cool water and the prospect of washing my grimy body had begun to excite me. I was dirty and sweaty and a razor cut on my finger looked like it was getting infected. I had figured it was about nine miles total to Cherry Lake Dam and hopefully I would meet someone there or on the way. If Jon or Tomoko had taken the car I didn't know what I would do but at least I'd be closer to people who could help me. I wasn't accomplishing anything on the ridge. If a search party came along all I could tell them is that I hadn't seen Tomoko.

There was an element to this whole thing that didn't seem real. It was like a television program or movie. These kinds of things don't happen to me. I was a national sales manager of a men's apparel company for crying out loud. What was I even doing here? What motivates people to take risks? Why do some people go on bus tours, stop at motel chains, and eat at hotel restaurants or fast food establishments while others sail around the world on small boats, go hiking or rafting or skydiving? I was actually bewildered to find myself so far from help and possibly in harm's way. And this was a vacation, a vacation that I had chosen for myself.

In my case I think I was looking to escape the world of accumulation and luxury. I thought it would be a worthwhile experience to live in nature and rely on myself rather than a variety of electronic conveniences. I wanted to test myself in a natural and possibly hostile environment thinking that it would help me develop my character. I absolutely needed to be immersed in nature and beauty. Having been raised in midtown Manhattan, I took every opportunity to get far away from civilization, surround myself with natural beauty, and be forced to rely on my own abilities.

I finished the lemonade around 7:30. Now an hour had gone by, and I allowed myself to fix a bowl of cereal. The milk powder we had packed with it didn't taste at all bad when water was added. I was watching my water supply very carefully. I had about a cup and a half, maybe less, in the bota bag, two cups in one bottle and a full quart in another bottle. I wanted to have at least a quart with me if I headed for the lake the next day. That meant I could only have three more cupfuls that day. I needed to take it relatively easy and stay out of the sun in order to reduce my dehydration. There were a few more carrots, but they would probably be dried out. To occupy myself during the afternoon, I planned to select items to bring with me the next day and to pack them.

My mind kept drifting to Tomoko. Memories of things we had done together kept inserting themselves, little things that wouldn't mean anything to anyone else. I wondered if Tomoko would even remember those particular events and conversations. It's funny how in human experience we can be present for the same event or conversation and remember them totally differently. I guess you could call it the Rashomon effect. Deep down, I didn't really know what Tomoko thought of me. Obviously I was her close friend, but did she have any ill feelings about my refusing to sleep with her? If she could go back in time and choose her behavior again would she play it out the same way? Would I? I hadn't seriously thought about it until now. I had never second guessed myself and this didn't seem to be an appropriate time.

After days of hard, hot, climbing, carrying a pack that kept driving me into the ground, fighting off insects, worrying about Jon and Tomoko, protecting my food from animals, being totally alone and wondering if I would be rescued, I was totally weary, mentally, physically, and emotionally. I felt a sudden and urgent need to rest my mind and my body. I found a comfortable spot under a tree, far from the bees, and I closed my eyes.

In those days I knew nothing about meditation. The word itself conjured up strange people chanting on a mountaintop in India. But at that moment I fell into a trance-like state. My mind cleared. All my fears, anger, and frustrations fell away. A sudden calmness pervaded me and I felt in total harmony with my surroundings. I no longer felt compelled to fight the perceived obstacles and dangers. I recognized a very natural and constant order. The flies, bees, mosquitoes, and bears had always lived there. The trees, rocks, sun, wind, midday heat and evening cool are part of the life of our planet. I was the element out of place. I was an intruder in this world. I became more aware and appreciative of the world outside myself that always exists. I had a tremendous realization that there was a natural harmony there in the mountains, and everywhere, and that I was, in fact, part of it. For the first time in my life I felt that I was truly a part of God's universe. It was a very special moment for me and I've never forgotten it.

In fact, it was the first of many subsequent meditations. That one came along naturally and without warning, but I was so influenced by the power and truth of it that I have continually tried to simulate and duplicate the experience. I long for the arrival of insights like that. They would be life transforming. To simulate those circumstances I sit in a comfortable chair, draw the drapes, disconnect the telephone, concentrate on my breathing and relax my body. In effect I am trying to unlearn the traditional forms of prayer that I have been taught and learned so well. I no longer try to talk to God, asking Him for something like Tomoko's rescue. If I really believe that God is a superior being or energy or presence and is omniscient, what sense does it make for me to tell it my problems? It knows my problems by definition. What kind of hubris would I be guilty of if I prayed to God to single me out and help me with my problems? In my reality it, God, doesn't know of my problems because it doesn't know anything. It doesn't care about anything. "Know" and "care" are human verbs that we ascribe to "God," like "Him," "Father" and "Lord" are made-up nouns. My superior being just is. I don't matter to it. I'm not important to it because nothing is important to something that doesn't judge. If I gave up asking God to let the New York Yankees beat the Boston Red Sox just this one time, and I did relinquish that form of prayer, then how could I ask Him to rescue Tomoko?

The revelatory experience on that mountain showed me that listening was more important than talking to my idea of God. The lesson was that I should quiet myself, let my picayune personal thoughts drift out of my consciousness and then after I unblock, get in touch with the deepest part of my consciousness. I should eliminate all talking, thinking, doing, and open myself up to God or the energy that I believe is always around me. I should be aware and receptive. In a way it's a self-calming exercise. I don't believe that there is a God, like a radio, who only turns on when I set something in motion.

Meditation has become very important in my life and I doubt that it would exist for me had it not been for that moment on the mountain. From time to time I still have to remind myself to relax, to stop fighting insignificant obstacles that are merely my perceptions, and to be aware of and to fit into the ubiquitous natural harmony.

I think it was Marcel Proust who said, "The real voyage of discovery consists not in seeking new landscapes but in having new eyes." I emerged from my meditation with new eyes.

This revelatory experience probably lasted 20 to 30 minutes. Then I returned to the rugged world of the Sierras and resumed my whistle blowing and name shouting.

It was 9:10 so I allowed myself an almost dried up carrot and a few sips of water. I thought I heard something unusual, jumped up, blew my whistle, listened, but heard nothing in return. Was I imagining things now? Probably an animal that I had frightened off. I thought about my four-inch knife, which wouldn't have been any help in an unfriendly encounter with an animal. I had covered up the stools around my tent with dirt so whatever animal was responsible wouldn't think that it was his personal dumping ground and develop a habit.

Every so often a plane flew overhead, but was so high I didn't think that it could be in a search pattern.

The louder buzzing of flies almost replaced the whining of mosquitoes. It was a welcome relief. The flies didn't bite. But the mosquitoes never left me completely alone.

My thoughts always returned to Tomoko and Jon. I knew my feelings for Jon were changing. Much of my respect for him had been for his professionalism, work ethic, and apparent inner strength. Now I was wondering if what I had seen over the years had all been an illusion. It's easy to be cool, calm, and collected if the stress in your environment is predictable and manageable. But when life throws you a curve, a situation outside of your normal pattern, then how do you react? Jon hadn't passed the test, in my opinion.

It's funny how one's impression of a person is often based on the last encounter. We tend to remember the clothes someone was wearing the last time we saw them. I don't want the last time I see friends and relatives to be in a bed in a hospital, because they tend to look frail and wan. I want to remember them as hale, hearty and robust. I couldn't get Jon's behavior the last time I saw him out of my mind. He was like a child totally lacking in self-discipline, seemingly without any inner strength. I had to instruct him in every phase of our rescue plan and then motivate him into action. He had totally lost his self-starting ability.

In any case I hoped he was well and had arrived safely at the dam. He hadn't taken any equipment for an overnight stay in the woods. I had the only tent and he had left his sleeping bag with me to save weight. All the fears I had for Tomoko were now applicable to him. He was susceptible to falling, breaking a bone, suffering from hypothermia, snakes, animals. I wondered what thoughts had run through his mind on his rush back. He must have worried about life without Tomoko. I imagined him thinking of his children, and how they would fare without their mom—and how he would take care of them—and how it would affect his damn research. I even wondered if this experience would help to uncover a hitherto unknown feeling that perhaps he really did have a deep-seated love for his wife.

I wondered if he had guilt feelings, and if I did. I thought about how this whole episode could have been prevented. Certainly we should have used our whistles more frequently and never roamed beyond hearing range. And we shouldn't have left the trail to go cross-country. The larger and much more significant issue is that we never should have planned such an ambitious trip. We three weren't experienced enough to make wise decisions, and we weren't in physical shape to carry the heavy packs and negotiate the rugged terrain.

But my job was to focus on the next day. I made a list of what I wanted to carry with me. I decided to leave by eight in the morning. That would give me 12 hours of daylight and a good margin of visibility in case I got lost or tired. Even if it took longer than I thought to get to the dam, the moon would provide decent light for about three hours until around 11:00 p.m. I was hoping to encounter other hikers along the way and get some kind of help. If you're wondering about cell phones, they hadn't been invented and I doubt if we would have carried them anyway. That kind of convenience was more like something we were trying to avoid than embrace.

But all my careful planning turned out to be unnecessary as the next sequence of events completely changed the profile of our trip.

Nine

At around 11:45 I was puttering with the packs when suddenly I heard a whistle coming from way down the hill and well into the woods. After all the whistle blowing I had done without an answer, this unsolicited sound was startling. I wondered if I was imagining the sound but it seemed so real. I whistled back. No answer. I waited. Another whistle from the woods. I blew my whistle. It answered. I blew again. Another answer. I yelled, "JON!" actually hoping that Tomoko would respond. Jon yelled, "HANK." At least I knew he was okay. But what about Tomoko? Jon yelled, "I'm coming, Hank." Then Tomoko's little voice, "I'm coming too." So they were both okay. I collapsed, crying uncontrollably. Jon's whistle interrupted me and I snapped back to reality. They still hadn't sighted me through the thick woods and needed to hear a locating whistle. I stopped crying and blew and blew and blew until they emerged from the trees.

I was wearing a blue nylon jacket over a sweatshirt for protection from the cold and bugs. "A little blue figure on a hill," is how Tomoko described me. Moments later Tomoko and I were hugging, and then I resumed my crying. I held her close, anxious to assure myself that she wasn't an apparition. What a feeling! A live, solid, healthy Tomoko. I thought the misadventure was finally over. Except it turned out that a new one was just starting.

First, I wanted to hear all the details of what had happened to Tomoko and Jon. No time for that now, according to Jon. We had to pack up everything and break camp as quickly as possible because, as Jon put it, we had to hurry and join up with "the two little boys and the mule train." That turned out to be two 12 year old boys from the pack station at Cherry Lake with five horses, two for them, three for us, and two mules to carry our packs. Jon said it was a simple 20 minute cross-country walk to the horses followed by a ten-mile ride to Cherry Lake Dam.

We quickly dismantled my tent and threw all of our belongings into the three packs. At this point it didn't matter what went where. It didn't take long to restore the area to its original state. As I prepared to follow Tomoko down the hill, I took a last look at the big tree where the packs had lain for three days and glanced quickly around the area.

I had a sudden and unexplained reluctance to leave. This was a sacred and special place for me, the site of an important revelation. This was where I had learned one of the most important lessons of my life. I had arrived here exhausted and angry at our stupidity for taking a cross-country route. When Tomoko disappeared and Jon left to obtain help, I was scared, apprehensive, insecure and lonely. In the following three days I had experienced a wide range of emotions as I faced the likelihood of Tomoko's death and Jon's predictable reactions, and the reality of the persistent onset of mosquitoes, ants, flies, bees, and bears. I had even feared for my own life. Then, without warning, a powerful peace had enveloped me. Simultaneously my mind released all anxious thoughts and a significant realization flooded my consciousness. Everything would be okay. I was okay. God had placed me in this environment so I could learn a critical lesson. Life on the planet was harmonious and interconnected. My arrogant insertion was selfish and disruptive. It was within my power to realize my oneness and adapt. And when I did, all perceived obstacles had disappeared and I learned to accept without wanting to "improve or correct."

With these memories, I lifted my pack and

headed down the mountain.

Tomoko finally assuaged my curiosity with a quick synopsis of what had happened after she had left us. She had gotten lost and just sort of wandered around feeling sorry for herself. She lost all sense of purpose and ceased looking for a trail and then, of course, is when she happened upon it. She knew that she had no chance of finding her way back to Jon and me so she just plopped down on the trail. Five hours later two men on horseback from the pack station rode by and picked her up. She remembered nothing about the hours she had spent on the trail. The riders took her to Cherry Lake Dam where she picked up the car keys we had hidden and drove to a lodge, whose name she didn't remember, and spent the night.

After Jon had left me, he took off at a fast pace down the hill. He covered the nine miles in five hours in a steady, panic-filled, whimpering, relentless jog that included a leap over a rattlesnake. He missed Kibbe Lake altogether even though he had a map, a compass, and the lake is four miles long!

I couldn't understand his jumbled explanation, but apparently Jon found Tomoko at the lodge and they had dinner together and stayed in the same bedroom. When I questioned each of them for more details I got incoherent answers. I think they were both so exhausted that their minds were a bit fragile.

Even though I was relieved to know that they were safe, I was surprised to notice a feeling of resentment come over me as I listened to their story. I had been out in the wilderness for two nights, worrying about bears and fighting off insects, boredom, and fear. While I was eating dried carrots, they were nice and cozy in a hotel dining room having dinner with silverware and napkins. While I had been yelling Tomoko's name and blowing my whistle, she had been in a lodge somewhere, probably with a shower handy.

Anyway, I was relieved and thrilled that they were okay and had found their way back to me. I was particularly happy that mules were waiting to carry my pack and a horse was there to transport my tired body.

So off we went for our 20-minute walk through the woods. But there was no such thing as a "simple 20 minute cross-country walk," at least not for us.

We followed Tomoko, who immediately lost her bearings. She turned to me for help. Having no idea where they had "parked" the horses, I was of no use at all. Jon volunteered that since they had come north to get me, all we had to do was head in a southerly direction, so we should follow him. He stepped off heading north. I called to him that if he wanted to go south he needed to turn around. He cursed me and told me that I didn't know what I was doing and was in no position to know where they had left the horses. I agreed with that part, but I sure knew the difference between north and south. We proceeded to argue like children. I was appalled to discover that he had left the compass in the car! With five horses, two mules, and two boys who were blowing whistles only a mile away, we spent the next THREE HOURS fighting our way exhaustedly through the heat and the bugs and around brambles, woods, marshes, and rocks. We blew our whistles and it turned out that the boys were blowing theirs, but we couldn't hear each other in the dense woods.

Jon and Tomoko were so tired physically and psychologically that they collapsed together on the ground and declared that they were done, finished. No more hiking, climbing, sweating for them today. I had to take control and yell at them to get them on their feet. I told them that this was a matter of survival and not to give in. Jon was amazingly testy, short-tempered, and despairing. I had never seen him like that. And he was still swearing that we were heading south when I knew we had been going north. I was absolutely sure that I was right on this point and the direction of the sun confirmed it. It was all I could do to keep them from losing total control of themselves.

I took charge and led them in a direction I

thought could be the right one. We still had to navigate through terribly dense underbrush and over large boulders but eventually we did find the trail. Immediately Jon fell on the ground and started crying uncontrollably. It was disheartening to watch his back heaving as gut-wrenching sobs racked his body. I had never seen an adult cry like that and I certainly didn't expect it from him. I left Tomoko to console him and walked up a nearby hill to see a gorgeous panoramic view of Cherry Lake and the dam at the south end. It took my breath away.

When I had had my fill of the view I returned to my friends. They both had agreed that the boys and the horses were about a mile up the trail and asked me if I would go by myself and find them. They didn't think they could make it. I took a bota bag of water and headed off. About a mile and a half later my whistle blasts were answered and I homed in on the boys. When I found them they were both smoking the last of a pack of homemade cigarettes and lounging on the ground. They reminded me of characters out of an *Our Gang* comedy. I introduced myself as the third person in our group and we agreed to immediately set off down the trail to pick up Jon and Tomoko.

I am reminded of the admonition, don't send a boy to do a man's job. These kids were way over their heads trying to control five horses, two mules, and themselves. The ride back to the pack station became a comedy of errors, except it wasn't funny at the time. I helped them load two of our backpacks in one mule's side packs and an air mattress, sleeping bag, tent and the third pack onto the second mule. Not knowing how to ride, I picked the most arthritic looking horse and hoisted myself up. When my feet were in the stirrups my knees were by my chest. I asked my guides to lower the stirrups but they didn't know how.

We started our short journey to hook up with Jon and Tomoko and were delighted to quickly come upon a small stream. As we stopped we almost lost one of the boys who became severely tangled among the horses and their reins. Hearing music of their own, the horses simultaneously started to circle wildly on the narrow trail. I was terrified that I'd be thrown off and trampled. Thick clouds of dust were circling in the air. Mongolians tell a story that if the dust kicked up by horses falls on you, it will bring you prosperity. If it's true, I should become very, very rich. The boys tried their best to stop the dance but it ended only when the horses got tired or bored.

We finished the one-and-a-half-mile trip to where Jon and Tomoko had collapsed and loaded the remaining gear onto the other mules. The trip to the pack station should have been simple and routine. All we had to do was follow the trail back, but as we were en route all of our gear slipped off the second mule and we had to rein in the horses and repack. Farther along, one of the boys and his saddle slid off a horse. We couldn't control our horses well enough to wait for him.

About a mile from the pack station, the horses, again hearing music of their own, started running toward home. No amount of "whoa"ing or rein pulling on our part had any effect. I held on for dear life and couldn't believe the pounding my butt and other more sensitive parts of my body were taking.

It seems funny to say but I prayed for a quick deliverance from my rescue.

As we approached the horses' home base they took off at a very fast, uncontrollable pace. I just hung on and tried to maintain my center of balance somewhere on the saddle. The three of us arrived at the pack station where steadier hands took hold of the reins and helped us dismount. I tried to stand on my quivering legs. The high stirrups and merciless pounding made it impossible for me to stand on my own for at least half an hour.

The boys arrived with the mules and our gear about an hour later and we thanked everyone and paid them for their efforts.

It always amazes me how, although we Americans all live in the same country, we have a such a wide variety of backgrounds. Those men and boys were as alien to us as if they were from a foreign country. I was 3,000 miles from home. I doubt if they had ever ventured more than a hundred from theirs. And where the three of us were college educated, they probably had never been inside a high school. I know I'm making a judgment based on appearances, but if you could have seen them and listened to them speak, you might agree. But I'm sure, to them, we were the misfits, the alien city slickers. I love traveling in the United States. We have so many people who can teach us so much about our country and about ourselves.

It was now about 8:00 p.m. and we didn't have the motivation or the strength to set up a campsite so we followed directions given to us at the pack station to a hotel called Evergreen Lodge. There, we rented a cabin with three cots and no running water. We went to a central dining area where we sat down at a table, were served by a waitress, and if I remember correctly, ordered one each of everything on the menu. After dinner we had a welcome, but rather chilly, shower in the communal bath house and quickly retired.

Part 3

Bears

"There was no doubt in our minds that these bears were staking us out and preparing an attack on our food after dark."

Ten

Sunday morning we felt much better. After taking turns standing under the cold trickle that was billed as the public shower, we had a full breakfast in the dining room served by the matronly lady in jeans and boots who had waited on us the previous evening. It wouldn't surprise me to learn that she was the wife of one of the men at the pack station. She was welcoming and warm and spoke without any semblance of grammar.

We were faced with a big decision. Do we pack it all in now and head home or do we continue our trip? Surprisingly it didn't take long to decide that we all wanted to continue. Despite being physically exhausted and emotionally drained, it was our vacation and we had planned for the better part of a year. There was an unspoken thought that if we went home then it would be a retreat that we would always regret. We didn't want to think of ourselves as quitters.

After cleaning up we drove to the Hetch Hetchy Reservoir and parked by the dam. It took us an hour to resort our equipment and organize our backpacks.

Explorers, soldiers, and tourists who had seen the Hetch Hetchy Valley prior to the damming of the Tuolumne River reported that it rivaled Yosemite Valley in natural beauty and grandeur. It lies about 20 miles north by northwest of Yosemite Valley at an elevation of 4,000 feet. The meandering river has created meadows where an incredible array of wild flowers thrives. Depending on the altitude and the season, one can enjoy the colors and aromas of lupine, shooting star, cow parsnip, mariposa lily, helianthella, mountain misery, mustang clover, larkspur, camas, cranesbill geranium, tiger lily, and many more. Surrounding the meadows are thick stands of Digger, Ponderosa, Jeffrey, and Lodgepole Pines. Singleleaf Pinyon, Black Cottonwood, Klamath Plum and a variety of firs add to the wonderful variety of vegetation in the area.

Almost from its discovery, Hetch Hetchy has been a battleground between the city of San Francisco and environmentalists. In the 1880s San Francisco's leaders started looking for sources of water in the High Sierra. They focused on the Tuolumne River and the idea was immediately circulated that if the valley was flooded and the river dammed, the water could be diverted to become part of the municipal water supply. Many San Franciscans expressed the idea that there were, in fact, two equally beautiful valleys. If one was dammed and radically changed, so what? There would still be one to utilize as a source for city water and the other for visiting and enjoying the scenery.

Strong opposition from the Sierra Club and its president John Muir, and from Secretary of the Interior, Ethan Allen Hitchcock, was enough, in the initial phases, to ward off developers.

In 1903 support for a dam became more focused when San Francisco Mayor James Phelan officially proposed damming the valley. The San Francisco earthquake and fire of 1906 didn't help the environmentalist cause as it promptly renewed calls for enlarging the city's water supply. By 1908, 86 percent of San Francisco's voters approved the funding of $600,000 to purchase the "lands, rights, and claims" of Hetch Hetchy. In 1913, the environmentalists lost the battle and the war. Congress passed the Raker Act dedicating Hetch Hetchy to San Francisco and allowing the flooding of the Hetch Hetchy Valley. President Woodrow Wilson signed it into law on December 19, 1913.

Many people who knew John Muir thought that his death the following year was due to his great despair and frustration at losing his long fight to maintain the area in its natural form. He had referred to the valley as "a wonderfully exact counterpart of Yosemite Valley" and "… a grand landscape garden, one of nature's rarest and most precious mountain temples."

Between 1914 and 1923, a gravity arch concrete dam was built, rising 312 feet above the original riverbed. We parked our car by the O'Shaugnessy Dam prior to starting the second phase of our hike. The dam creates a reservoir with 360,360 acre-feet of capacity. (An acre-foot is one foot of water covering one acre, equal to 43,560 feet.) An aqueduct carries the water 172 miles to the city. The reservoir, which is fed by snow melt from Yosemite hills and mountains, extends eight miles into the valley. Two waterfalls pour into the north end, the Tueeulala, also known as Tuella (1,000 feet), and Wapama (1,500 feet). The former was completely dried up when we arrived.

There have been many attempts to have the dam removed and the valley restored to its original state. The most notable were in 1963 and 1987. In 1963, Secretary of the Interior Stewart L. Udall appointed Professor A. Starker Leopold to head a wild life commission. It was called the Wildlife Management Advisory Board and it issued The Leopold Report calling for the restoration of all of the national parks to their original state. This was a thinly veiled plea for the restoration of the Hetch Hetchy Valley by destroying the dam. No action was taken as a result of this report.

In 1987, President Ronald Reagan's Secretary of the Interior, Donald Hodel, declared that San Francisco should look elsewhere for its water. Again no action was taken.

The effort to restore the Hetch Hetchy Valley continues. In September 1997, a new group called the Sierra Club Hetch Hetchy Restoration Task Force was organized. At this writing, in early 2000, the directors are in the process of trying to establish non-profit status to be better able to appeal to organizations and individuals for funding. Their ultimate goal is to decommission the O'Shaugnessy Dam and restore the flooded valley to its original state.

There will be many difficulties, not the least of which will be the negotiation with San Francisco city and county officials. There are a number of electrical, water power generation, and revenue issues to be resolved.

When we arrived at the reservoir we were stunned by its inherent beauty. All around us were rounded granite domes that led directly into the water. (They originally had risen from the valley floor, but now that it was flooded, it appeared that the granite was growing out of the lake.) As at Cherry and Kibbe Lakes, the dramatically lowered water line was evidenced by a wide bleached band on the granite surrounding the reservoir.

Two hikers asked us where we were headed and when we told them, warned us to watch out for bears in that area. They had done everything possible to protect their food but had lost it all to the crafty animals. With no food, they had to abort their trip and were going home.

We started our hike by crossing the dam at 2:30 p.m. and then proceeded up the lovely terraces of the reservoir. We planned to have a swim at Tuella Falls, but it had dried up and we passed the area without even noticing it. We did stop at Wapama Falls and took a lovely protracted dip thinking we were at Tuella Falls. Oh well, with all the mistakes we made on this vacation, this was the most innocuous. The water was cool, clear, and refreshing. Next stop was Tiltill Creek, which on the map showed two separate and distinct branches. When we arrived, one was completely dry and the other was barely flowing. One of the things we had learned, and the lesson was constantly being confirmed, was that most of the streams listed as intermittent were dry. As droughts go, this was a bad one.

Around 7:30, with a half hour of daylight to spare, we neared Rancheria Creek, which apparently always has an abundance of water. It is the beneficiary of runoff from snow melt from two of the three zones above us, the Canadian and the Hudsonian. The highest zone, the Arctic-Alpine, doesn't supply runoff because the winds, which often reach 120 miles an hour, blow the snow off the bald, treeless granite before it can settle and harden.

We heard the water before we saw it. The waterfalls made a rushing sound that penetrated the woods. You can't imagine how relieved we were to know that we would finally be able to camp near water. Our first sight of the creek was a large cascading fall pouring over smooth, polished rock. At the foot of the falls, the creek ran through layered granite with carved out rounded holes that had filled with water and had formed small pools. The power of the rushing water created the illusion that we were watching eons of gradual erosion occurring before us as we watched. Our senses were instantly and fully engaged. We heard the splashing water, felt a wave of cooler air, and were awestruck by the physical beauty of the area. This was the place for us to camp!

In the fading light we set up a campsite within sight and sound of a lovely and powerful waterfall. I found an elevated shelf on which to pitch my tent and Jon and Tomoko laid their large, orange, ground cloth next to it. After rolling out our sleeping bags we rummaged through our packs to gather food for dinner. It seemed as if all of the trees were evergreen so we set out in three different directions to collect fallen pine logs and limbs for a fire. As we occupied ourselves with all of our chores, we had no idea that we were being watched.

Eleven

"Is that a bear over there?" I looked in the direction that Tomoko was pointing. It was indeed a bear and he was looking straight at us. He was about 50 meters away and was lumbering in a counter-clockwise circle around our newly formed campsite. Then I saw another, and another. It turned out that he had brought an entourage of five adults and one cub. They were all slowly circling our campsite and regarding us with evident interest. Our first thought was to build up the fire and act naturally. The rangers at Groveland had warned us that there were lots of bears in the park and that they would be interested in our food, not us. That little piece of information didn't reassure me at that moment. To tell it plainly, I was really scared. I had never seen bears without strong, iron bars between them and me and at Rancheria Falls there was nothing to protect us.

I've always been nervous around intoxicated people who behave irrationally but at least they are human and have some acquaintance with behavioral norms. Wild animals scare me because of their total unpredictability. I'm not familiar with their normal behavior and I don't understand how they think. I wondered if these bears would act as a group or individually. It occurred to me that they might attack us immediately to get us out of the way so they could get to the food, or they might avoid us in the daylight and try to get the food in the dark while we slept. There were lots of other possibilities, most of which made me very uneasy. In any case, it was very exciting to be so close to them in this setting and I wished that I knew more about them. As time passed, I learned.

The technical name for them is *ursus americanus*. Their more common name is the North American Black Bear, although not all the bears we encountered were black. On the east coast, bears are mostly black; but in the west, where we were, bears have a wide range of coat colors. The ones circling our camp were either black or various shades of brown. In the coming days and with their repeat visits, we actually identified them by giving them names based on their appearance, like Blackie, Brownie, Mr. Tan.

Bears have carved out a large area for themselves from Northern Mexico to Alaska and across to the Great Lakes and the Appalachians. They used to inhabit most of the forested areas of North America but as the forests were cut down the bears had to retreat to the surviving wooded areas. Bear populations are diminishing in proportion to their food supply. As people continue to cut down and develop natural forested areas, bears are forced to raid beehives, garbage dumps, orchards, live stock, and campsites for food. Some humans find this behavior aggravating and economically undesirable so they shoot the bears. This, obviously, is not helping the species to thrive. In addition, bears are valued by various cultures for their gall bladders and their paws. Hunters kill bears, remove these parts, and leave the rest of the animal to rot on the ground. In the natural order of things bears only live about 32 years.

Bears breed only from May to July. The gestation period is 210-215 days and then the female gives birth to three or fewer cubs in January or February. The cubs stay in the den with their mothers until April or May and then stick close to her for the next 1 ½ to 2½ years. The cubs are tiny at birth, weighing between 7.8 and 10.4 ounces. The one regarding us was definitely on the mature side. The weight of adult and baby bears corresponds pretty closely to humans. I haven't heard of anyone inventing fertility pills for bears, so the typical female will have only six to eight cubs in her lifetime. Where food supplies are dwindling there will be fewer. In the west, most bears don't begin breeding until they are three to four years old.

Bears are omnivorous although they prefer nutritious, delicious vegetation like young shoots, tubers, bulbs, nuts, and berries. They also feed on grubs, carrion, young hoofed animals (farmers and ranchers are well aware of this), and fish. From all the documentaries I've seen on public television and The Discovery Channel I've drawn the conclusion that salmon is their favorite fish. A bear needs about 11-18 pounds of food a day. I weigh just a little bit less than an average adult female bear. Even when I'm at an all -you-can-eat buffet table I eat a lot less than she does, but I'm not nearly as active.

Adult females weigh about 200 pounds with a range of 155 to 265 pounds in the east. They're smaller in the west, usually 100-200 pounds. The average western female weighs 145 pounds. Add 10-50 percent for the males. Weight depends on food supply and the abundance of energy rich acorns and beechnuts in the east accounts for the larger sizes there. The largest recorded male was 600 pounds. I could swear that all the bears we encountered were world record males. When they are circling your campsite and looking straight into your eyes they attain world record stature. Actually they do resemble small grizzly bears in many ways but there are no grizzlies in Yosemite now. The last one was hunted down in the 1920s.

Northern populations of black bears den for about half the year, after which they need to regain their weight. They've been roaming ever-increasing areas foraging for the richest possible food. It's not unheard of for female bears to travel an area up to 36 square miles looking for a hearty dinner. Males have been known to range areas up to six times larger. Because of the long winters and colder weather in the north, food is scarce and slow growing. Not all females find enough energy-rich food to be ready for mating, putting an additional burden on the males to find food and suitable females.

If you measure them from head to tail, (needless to say, we didn't) you'd find most of the bears are from four to six feet long. Their shoulder height is from 31 to 37 inches.

American Black Bears are promiscuous. One litter may have more than one father but from what I could tell, the cubs are much less concerned with this than humans are. The mother will vigorously defend her litter so we quickly identified the adult walking closest to the cub. With food growing more and more scarce and with females only giving birth to a maximum of eight cubs in a lifetime, every unnatural death, for example, humans shooting them, is a significant loss to the bear population.

We quickly noticed individual personalities, some were much more aggressive than others. Some were so timid they never ventured past an imaginary perimeter they seemed to have drawn around our campsite. Others were more playful and seemed less interested in us. I guessed they were younger. We feared and respected all of them.

During the afternoon, while searching for stones and firewood, we had spotted two rattlesnakes sunning themselves on the rock ledges. From then on we were very careful to look far in front of us and avoid crevices where rattlers could have been sleeping.

We decided that evening not to prepare a hot meal. We didn't want to tempt the bears with cooking aromas. Hot coffee topped off a cold dinner. In the remaining hour of light and well into dusk we gathered as much wood as we could for our fire, and rocks for hurling at the bears. We were careful to forage only in directions where we didn't see signs of life.

As evening settled in, we kept the fire roaring. If the more aggressive bears moved closer to us we banged our cutlery against our mess kits, making as much noise as we could. We also yelled and blew our whistles and threw small rocks and stones in their direction. All of these activities seemed to have the desired effect, as the bears would retreat into the darkness.

Although I'm aware that scientifically, darkness is just the absence of light, I think of it as something palpable. When I spend extended time outdoors, my awareness of the environment increases. Then I feel that "night" or "darkness" is a physical entity with its own identity that slowly eases into my world, invading from east to west as the sun retreats. I am vaguely conscious that I can see, touch, and feel the dark and the night. I think of "night" as being cool, damp, quiet and sensual while "day" is warmer, dryer and filled with the brighter sounds of life. With a campfire burning I have the sense that I am creating an atmosphere in limbo, somewhere between day and night, and I am thereby averting or warding off the impending physicality of night. Daylight and campfires were comforting and reassuring to me. At Rancheria Falls I had the feeling that the bears were moving in and out of different earthly atmospheres as they appeared and disappeared. Unfortunately they never stayed invisible for long, requiring us to keep our mess kits and rocks at the ready.

We amused ourselves by yelling insulting curses knowing they didn't understand. We made a game out of trying to compose what, at the time, seemed like clever phrases, such as "Come and get us you stupid pigs!"

After dinner we put all our food and items that might emit a tempting aroma into two large nylon stuff bags. Then we selected two pines growing close together. Jon climbed about ten feet up one of them and tossed a rope over a branch of the other. The food bag had been tied to this rope and we pulled it out so that it hung halfway between the trees. It was now four feet from each tree and ten feet above the ground. We used the same procedure for the second food bag using two trees not too close to the first pair. We regarded our handiwork with smug satisfaction, feeling sure that in the contest between the humans and the bears, we had scored one for the humans.

After dinner we stayed awake as long as we could, amusing ourselves by singing songs as we sat around the fire. Thinking it would be a good idea to keep the fire burning all night, we assigned ourselves alternating one-hour shifts to stay awake. After completing our plans, two of us went to sleep, leaving the first "guard" to do whatever was necessary to keep the fire roaring and the bears away. Unfortunately we were all so tired that by 2:00 a.m. all three of us were asleep. The fire also had retired for the night. At one point I heard a bear's claws scratching on one of the trees. I got up and scared it away. I was not at all happy to see that it had been climbing on one of the pines from which our food was suspended. The next morning the bears were nowhere to be seen.

"The food bag had been tied to this rope and we pulled it out so that it hung halfway between the trees. It was now four feet from each tree and ten feet above the ground."

Twelve

The first thing we did upon rising was to look for our two food bags. Our main supply was gently swaying where we had left it high above the ground. The smaller bag was on the ground under the tree. It had been ripped and shredded into tiny pieces of bright blue nylon. There were remnants of all the contents spilled and scattered over a wide area. It was obvious that the bears had climbed the tree and torn the bag down. The bears had then proceeded to feast on Sanka, Tang, milk powder, sugar, toothpaste, and soap liquid, supplemented by side dishes of suntan lotion and Vaseline.

Bear claws grow as long as 2.4 inches, (I've researched this, I wasn't the one who did the measuring), which enables them to be versatile tree climbers. Not only did they climb the tree from which we strung our food, I really believe they untied our knots. When we closely examined the remains of our food bag on the ground we could see that the attendant ropes were not cut, torn, or bitten in any way. Perhaps years of park rangers feeding the bears to attract tourists had made them more savvy than their wilder cousins.

I'm guessing that if you asked the average *ursus americanus* what meal he'd like to find in a camper's stuff bag, he wouldn't include suntan lotion, Vaseline and soap liquid in his answer. Logic dictated that if they had gone to so much trouble for such an unbalanced diet they would redouble their efforts this night for our main food supplies.

The fact that our handiwork of suspending the food proved to be inadequate was a significant blow to our self-esteem and morale. It was also a wake up call to us that the bears were more aggressive and talented than we had anticipated. We had done everything the rangers had instructed, and then some, as the stuff bags were suspended farther off the ground than our directions warranted. Jon had climbed, limb by limb, to get about ten feet off the ground. The bears could obviously climb higher than we could so we had no idea how to protect the food in the future. Losing the balance of our food would mean the end of the trip. The novelty of the bears quickly wore off and the reality of our situation set in.

We had noticed that the bears appeared at our campsite around four in the afternoon, had stayed with us most of the night, and were gone by morning. They only attacked our food supplies after dark and when we were not awake standing vigil. We knew that if I hadn't heard the scratching of the claws on the nearby tree in the middle of the night, we would have lost the second bag too.

With all of our concerns about the bears' appetites, we still hadn't eaten anything ourselves, so we built up the fire and cooked a large breakfast of pancakes and coffee. We had decided to spend several days in this lovely spot so we planned to take some time enhancing our campground. But before we could devote ourselves to other projects, we had a more important issue to resolve. Since all of us were professional business people, used to attending and conducting meetings, it was not out of character for us to have a formal meeting in the wilderness, so shortly before 9:30 a.m., under a cloudless sky, in a remote area of Yosemite National Park, three somber citizens of the world gathered for a meeting of great import. Present were, Jonathan Roberts, Ph.D., a full professor at a prestigious west coast business school, Tomoko Roberts, D.V.M., owner and operator of a successful veterinary medicine practice, and Henry

Stark, B.A., national sales manager and adjunct faculty member. The agenda of the seminar was simple but critical. It could have been titled, "Rancheria Creek North American Black Bear Management." Eavesdroppers at the conference would have been impressed with the seriousness of the discussion and the gravitas of the participants. At the end of almost an hour of heated discussion, six principles of bear management had been agreed to:

1. More rocks were to be gathered for hurling in the bears' direction.

2. Large logs and small branches were to be located and carried or dragged to the campsite for all-night fire burning.

3. Metal mess kits, cooking spoons, and whistles were to be stored in easy view of all campers for immediate accessibility if scary noise making was required.

4. The remaining food and other aromatic items were to be divided into three equal piles.

5. Each pile was to be shoved into a nylon stuff bag.

6. Each stuff bag was to be suspended as high off the ground and as far from the supporting trees as possible for a period of 24 hours per day, unless the contents were currently in use.

When there was no more coffee in the pot, we

adjourned the meeting and proceeded to divide our remaining food into three equal lots and put them into separate bags. Our idea was that it would take three separate attacks to destroy all of our food and that we would hear the first one in time to scare the bears away before they could get to the second and third bags. Before we started any other activity we suspended each of the bags from pairs of trees near our site. The choice of trees was a compromise: on the one hand, close enough so we would hear bear claws scratching; and on the other hand, far enough away so that the animals were not lured into our immediate campground.

The next chore was to gather a much larger quantity of wood than we had assembled the night before. It was easy to locate trees that had fallen and with all three of us dragging them, we were able to steer several to our campsite. We arranged them around the fire pit where they became benches for us to sit on during the day and were to serve as firewood during the night. The plan was to start a fire under one end of the tree, and as it burned, we would continue to push the rest of the log into the fire. It should take most of the night for the huge log to burn. We also collected many more rocks for hurling at the bears.

After cleaning our cookware and mess kits, it was time to attend to our own personal cleanliness so we headed for the base of the waterfall. The falling water had scoured the surface of the rocks so that they were smooth and slippery. Looking at the water tumbling onto the smooth rocks we all saw only one thing, water slide!

I have no idea how long we spent crouching among the rocks watching the water pour down in front of us or how many times we slid, with the water, down the rocks. But I do know we would have continued a lot longer if we had had bathing suits that could have supported our vulnerable body parts. None of us wanted to deal with wet underwear so when the pain outweighed the fun, we headed back to the campsite to prepare lunch.

The three food bags that we had strung up were still in place. They represented a bit of surrealism in the remote wilderness. From afar we couldn't see the supporting ropes, so the bright blue bags, suspended in the air between the trees, looked like balloons that were flying in to meet us. Having had the foresight to pack all of our lunch food and supplies in one bag, we were able to leave two of the bags in position as we dined on cheese, sandwiches, and candy. None of us was masochistic enough to want to bounce on the rocks of the waterfall in the afternoon so we enjoyed a long walk, explored the area, and finally, sunned on the rocks.

The sun bathing abruptly ended as large, dark,

dense cumulonimbus clouds drifted over us. There was an accompanying chill in the air and we quickly retreated to our campsite. I rigged a poncho over my tent to provide added rain protection but it was a false alarm. The clouds continued to drift over and away from us and the drought continued unbroken

As four o'clock approached we anticipated the arrival of the bears, so we lowered the food bags and sorted things out for dinner. Although we were apprehensive about tempting them with dinner aromas, we didn't want to have a second cold dinner in a row. We decided to build a large fire and cook dinner as quickly as possible. Freeze dried meals were basically cooked in pouches which mostly contained the odors and we fixed a fine repast of chicken with peanuts, coconut, and raisins. A post prandial cognac helped to stiffen our resolve for our evening encounter.

The bears arrived on schedule. This time they approached much closer to our campsite. It was almost as though the word had gone out that three new greenhorn campers had brought in a fresh supply of food. There was no doubt in our minds that these bears were staking us out and preparing an attack on our food after dark. It was terribly depressing to know that we were out there alone, in a remote area of the wilderness, trying to prevent wild animals from stealing our food. This could have been a life or death issue for the bears, and for us, as we were dealing with issues like hunger and survival. All we could do was play a game of keep-away. We were totally defenseless if the bears decided to attack us, the keepers of the food. We did everything we could to keep our spirits up in the face of these thoughts.

Thirteen

Over a period of almost 80 years, a motley combination of self-serving, thoughtless, and ignorant human beings has turned nature upside down in Yosemite National Park. Bears living in the park in the 1920s behaved very differently from the bears inhabiting it today. Fortunately, to understand how the natural order was changed is to know that it is not irreversible.

Appearances now suggest that campers bring in comestibles that have been prepared and packaged for humans, only to have bears crave these products, raid their campsites and steal the food. It didn't take long for both the human and the bear populations to begin believing that this was perfectly natural behav-

145

ior. In reality, it is not the least bit natural. It is important to remember that bears, without the presence of humans, eat indigenous vegetation like shoots, tubers, nuts, and berries for nutrition and energy. They don't have innate cravings for national branded items such as Tang, Sanka, and Vaseline. Nor do cubs emerge from the womb asking for Gouda cheese and soda crackers. Unfortunately, bears were led, step-by-step, into this routine to satisfy their basic hunger needs.

So, one might wonder, what has happened to the bears to make them depart from their instinctual proclivities and to become so aggressive with campers? Why have they become partially dependent on human food supplies that are carried into the wilderness and, concurrently, why have they lost some of their own hunter-gatherer instincts? Learning a bit about the history of the American Black Bear in Yosemite National Park provides answers to these and other related questions.

In 1923, The Yosemite National Park Company began a virtual training program for bears, which, in effect, taught them to raid campsites in the park. About a mile from Yosemite Lodge, a major destination for tourists, workers from the company erected a feeding platform overlooking a river. Floodlights were brought in and trained on the platform. Since bears were used to scavenging garbage from the lodge and therefore did not normally visit the area where the new platform had been constructed, workers poured oil on the hotel garbage to make it inedible. This had the effect of depleting one of the bears' regular sources of food. In a further enhancement of the program, it soon became part of the job description that wherever staff members found garbage or food of any kind, oil was to be poured on it and it was to be set on fire.

The next step was to collect fresh garbage and dump it on the feeding platform at regular hours. It didn't take long for the bears to learn to anticipate garbage dumping times and to visit the platform on schedule.

During this time, the United States government had been maintaining garbage dumps at national parks. At about the same time the Yosemite National Park Company was working on the feeding platform training program, the government closed a large garbage dump in the area. The bears, in effect, were being directed to feed at a) public campsites where the garbage was originating, and b) the feeding platform, its ultimate destination. It seems obvious that the bears were being trained by a commercial company abetted by a federal agency, the National Park Service, to engage in aberrant behavior.

Once the bears had accustomed themselves to

the feeding platform and figured out the feeding schedule, the floodlights were illuminated. Aggressive marketing commenced and it wasn't long before tourists were being bussed to the area to see the "Bear Shows."

But the bears were not the only creatures being trained. The tourists were also being educated, albeit subliminally, to accept as fact that bears were domesticated pets, not wild animals.

As an ever-increasing number of tourists arrived to watch the bear shows, the problems mounted. One legitimate question being raised was: Is the park being run for the enjoyment of the tourists or for the preservation and use by the native animals?

On July 16, 1929, an evening bear show attracted almost 2,000 people, driven to the area in 336 cars and four busses. Not coincidentally, that same year 81 people were treated at the valley hospital for bear-inflicted injuries.

It wasn't long before tourists became bolder and started feeding the bears themselves. Naturalists estimated that because of the artificial food supplies being brought in, the number of bears in the park had grown to four times what it would have been under normal conditions.

Conflicts quickly developed among the humans. Tourists loved the bears and wanted to visit with and feed them. Campers and residents feared and despised the bears and considered them a major nuisance. A love-hate relationship of the bears had already developed by the 1920s.

Contact between bears and humans became closer and more threatening as the feeding process developed. As tourists slowly drove around the park hoping to catch glimpses of the bears, the bears started approaching their cars looking for food. Visitors often left their vehicles to take a walk or a picture. Carelessly, they left food in the cars and neglected to close the windows and sometimes even doors. Damage to the cars ensued and lawsuits were threatened. Bears also broke into tents, suitcases, and housing. One wonders if the bears were attracting people or scaring them away. The more that humans intruded on the bear habitat, the more aggressive the bears got, and the greater the outcry to kill them. A mix of myth and fear became more prevalent than objective logic. A black bear had never killed a human being.

Tourists and campers even approached mother bears with their cubs in an effort to feed the cute, little, cuddly teddy bears. Protective mothers, not understanding human intent, attacked the tourists in order to defend their offspring. In turn, those female bears were hunted down as violent predators and killed.

I wonder why those people had been so stupid to try to feed bear cubs and their mothers in the wild? I'm also troubled that we killed the bears rather than punished the humans who invaded their environment and intruded in their lives? It seems clear that people encouraged bears to behave abnormally and then killed them because they did.

Conservationists had long suspected that sport hunters and ranchers were shooting bears with impunity. In 1973, government officials finally admitted that more than 200 bears had been killed in the park between 1960 and 1972. Many believed the toll had been a lot larger and that the killing had started much earlier.

After years of encouraging humans to interact with bears, the National Park Service was having difficulty managing both groups. In an effort to discourage human involvement, signs were erected reading, "CAUTION: DO NOT FEED THE BEARS FROM THE HAND." I am stunned by the mentality. "...FROM THE HAND?!" Several years later, in 1937, realizing that the signs were not effective, new warnings were posted, "DANGER: DO NOT FEED THE BEARS." (This is the same agency that started a "controlled burn" to clear underbrush near Los Alamos in May 2000. Three weeks later the conflagration had destroyed hundreds of homes and 48 thousand acres.)

The more contact humans had with bears, the more injuries occurred. In the autumn of 1940, the government finally abolished all bear shows in the park. But the bears never received the memo. Tourists were still encouraged to visit the park and feed the bears, and the bears continued to injure the tourists who invaded their sanctuaries.

People trained bears to come to feeding platforms for meals, and filled their cars, tents, and lodges with the tempting aromas of raw and prepared food. Then, because the National Park Service finally decided that their long-term bear/human management policies had been a failure and rescinded them, the authorities expected bears to suddenly avoid all human contact.

As Jon, Tomoko, and I sat around our campsite watching the bears circle, we were aware that these were the same bears, and their descendants, who had graduated from The National Park Service and Yosemite National Park Company training programs. They were now waiting for us to fall asleep so they could practice their well-developed skills and raid our prepared and packaged food.

We were not surprised to notice that there were more bear visitors on our perimeter than had been there the night before. It was hard to count them because they kept moving in and out of the trees but we thought there might have been about a dozen. We assumed that the bears had spent the day networking and that word of our presence, with our goodies, had spread.

We started a fire and gradually eased a large tree into it. When the end of the log was fully engaged we cooked our dinner, again avoiding any cooking aromas that might drive the bears into a feeding frenzy.

Before we were aware of the settling in of evening, it was dark. None of us had the courage, (or the stupidity?) to walk to the river to wash our mess kits but we didn't want to keep dishes with food particles too near us. We rinsed them with boiling water at our campsite and hoped we had washed most of the food away.

I learned later that it's a good idea to change clothing after cooking at a campfire. Food odors permeate clothes much as smoke does in a restaurant. It's just not a good idea to zip yourself into a sheer nylon tent in bear country smelling like a grilled pork chop.

As we were talking around the fire, Jon suddenly leaped up and shone a flashlight on one of the trees where a food bag was hung. A bear was halfway up the tree. We succeeded in frightening it off with a shower of rocks and as much noise as we could muster. We settled back into our talking/coffee drinking positions and in the light of our fire we immediately spotted another bear on the other side of our campsite. It couldn't have been more than 15 feet away. We hooted, banged, yelled, threw rocks, and shone flashlights. Again we succeeded in scaring the bear away. At the same time we were relieved to see the other bears in the area lumber out of sight.

This was getting as irritating as the hordes of mosquitoes we had faced. We could never relax; someone had to always be on guard. I could feel my stress level rising precipitously. How long would we be able to scare the bears away? When might they realize that we were paper tigers with no way of hurting them or preventing them from getting our food? Would they ever attack us, thinking that if they could get us out of the way there would be a clear path to all of our food?

That night we took turns standing guard and since we were more rested and more worried, there was no temptation for the guard to fall asleep. We made it through the night without losing anything but sleep.

Tuesday was a day of rest and fun, but a night of frustration. We risked a cooked breakfast, as the bears had never appeared in the morning. As soon as we had cleaned our mess kits in the river, we hung our food bags and gathered more wood and rocks.

By 10:00 we were able to head for the river for some needed relaxation. As we were sliding down the smooth polished rocks of the waterfalls we heard human voices. Being totally naked we ran as fast as we could to our jettisoned clothes and were barely dressed when a small group of Boy Scouts and their leader emerged from the woods. I think they were as happy to see us as we were to find human company. They were so cute competing with each other trying to tell us their bear stories. Their excitement bubbled over as they told us how they had lost all their food to wild bears the previous night. But for these intrepid campers, the trip was over.

In talking with the leader we learned that they had employed the same techniques trying to protect their food as we had, but for them, it hadn't worked. I wondered if their group had distracted some of the local bear population from our area and if their departure was going to mean more trouble for us. It was not a great leap in logic to posit that since the bears were able to climb the Boy Scouts' trees, they surely could climb ours. We were probably next on their agenda!

If this conversation seemed depressing, there at least was a silver lining around the cloud. The good news about the encounter for me was that the scout leader was a smoker. I was addicted to cigarettes at the time and had been carefully rationing them as, day by day, my stocks literally went up in smoke. I was in a state of mind, and so dependent, that I would have given up almost anything to get more cigarettes. As it happened, since the scout leader would be able to replenish his supplies in the relatively near future, I was able to successfully negotiate a trade of some of my fruit, candy, and nuts for his remaining packs.

Some may think this of no import, but for a dedicated smoker in the wilderness it was an important event. As I relate this incident I must admit that I am ashamed. I had allowed my value system to be corrupted. Food was critical in this situation and I shouldn't have traded it. Taking a more global point of view, even though it was my own personal ration that I gave away, I should have held on to it in case I needed to share it with my friends in an emergency.

Finally, what does it say about my character at that time to desperately want, need, and indulge in something that I knew was so detrimental to my health? Cigarettes, for me, shouldn't have been a necessity; they were a manmade product, which I could have chosen to renounce. I knew better, and I still didn't change my behavior. Perhaps it was a combination of a lack of willpower, inadequate self-discipline, or a false sense of my own indestructibility.

Thinking back, I believe there was also a strong element of believing it was "cool" to casually exhale plumes of smoke. I was much more a victim of marketing then than I am now. I had lulled my brain into allowing myself to believe smoking was a man's thing. Not just a man, but a macho, rugged, independent, man who really knew how to handle himself and appreciate the outdoors. In my mind I had become "the Marlboro Man." I never considered the facts, that I was inhaling into the only two lungs that I would ever have, a combination of burning paper and tobacco leaves with who-knows-what additives.

When I eventually gave up smoking, I did it "cold turkey." Why hadn't I done it then, when I was so keenly aware of the health risks? That was the time in my life when I was most appreciative of the clear mountain air and needed all the healthy lung capacity I could get for hiking.

The incident with the Boy Scout leader bothered me for months after the vacation was over. I didn't like to be dependent on anything or anyone. In analyzing my personality, I realized that anytime a stressful situation came up, my automatic response was to reach for a cigarette. Anytime coffee was served after a meal, I had the same reaction. Once I realized, about six months later, that I wasn't dealing with the stress on my own terms but depending on a cigarette, it was easy for me to quit smoking. So I credit that incident at Rancheria Falls for being a catalyst in a tremendous improvement in my physical health and self-esteem over the years.

The scouts had to leave after a short visit and it was back to business for us. A fire was started, a log pushed in, and another dinner cooked in a pouch. Somehow, all of our dinners were beginning to taste like soup or stew. We did the best we could rinsing off our mess kits, then strung up the food bags. We had already settled into a routine.

The bears made their daily appearance shortly after four. The scene would have been cute and funny if the situation hadn't been so frightening. That evening we were feeling more confident because of our success in preserving our two main bags of food the previous two nights. If we could keep the bears away then, why couldn't we do the same every night? Surely we were a lot sharper than a bunch of little kids in Boy Scout uniforms! It wasn't long before we realized that our confidence had really been self-deception.

"The food bags that we had strung up were still in place. They represented a bit of surrealism in the remote wilderness."

Fourteen

After dinner we sat around the fire enjoying coffee and cognac. We sang songs in strongly audible voices hoping to keep the bears away, (not because we couldn't sing on key, for all I know bears are tone deaf, but due to our loudness). Since we had plenty of wood and rocks, were tired from the day's activities, and had a bit of a buzz from the alcohol, we all decided to go to bed around 10:30. We were reasonably confident that our two remaining bags of food were safe because they had already survived two nights. We had them hanging in the same pines and they were swinging very high and far out from the trees.

During the night I imagined that I heard bear

noises but figured I was getting paranoid or was dreaming. Every once in a while I shined my flashlight in the appropriate direction but saw nothing. I glanced at Jon and Tomoko to see if they were noticing anything unusual but they were sawing logs, in a figurative sense, and I assumed that I was just hearing the popping of firewood.

At 12:40, Jon got up to relieve himself and routinely shone his light at the nearest food bag. He couldn't see it. It wasn't where it should have been. He woke me and told me about his awful discovery. I put on my boots and, from just outside my tent, peered through the dark. I couldn't see the bag either. A feeling of panic invaded me. We woke Tomoko. When she was ready, we each picked up a handful of rocks and moved closer to the first pair of trees. On the ground, next to the tree where it had hung, lay a badly ripped nylon bag. In fact, it was no longer a bag, just random bits of cloth. There were shredded Ziploc bags and plastic food containers strewn all over the immediate area. This was much worse than the first bag we had lost three days ago. None of us could have imagined such total destruction and we just stared at the remains wordlessly, each of us taking a moment trying to absorb the significance.

As if a lightning bolt hit us all at the same time, we thought of the other bag and ran to the other pair of trees to see if it was intact. It seemed to be. We decided to bring it down immediately to work with it and split its contents, but as we loosened the anchoring rope and lowered the bag, we could see that it, too, was ripped and empty.

In the dark it was difficult to tell what, if anything, had survived. We brought everything we could over to the light of the campfire and picked through it. All the while we were blowing our whistles, shouting, and throwing rocks at the ubiquitous bears who were observing us from the edge of the circle of light.

Deciding that it would be easier to sort through it in the morning daylight, we carried the remainder of the detritus to a rock ledge about ten feet away from the fire. Within five minutes a bear was working it over. We had never experienced a bear so close and it scared the daylights out of us. It was like they had declared war on us and were determined, no matter what, to get all our food. I think the taste and smell of the food they had already devoured had gotten the better of any cautionary instincts and emboldened them. Their new-found resolve and lack of fear was frightening to us.

We were successful in scaring away that bear, but we didn't want to risk any more encounters. We went to the ledge where we had placed the food remains and dumped everything over to the other side of the ledge. If the bears wanted our food, fine, they could have it. We had had enough! In our desperation we didn't think it was worth risking our lives for some half-eaten, filthy food. The rock ledge gave us considerable protection from the bears, and if all they truly wanted was the remains of our food, they could get to it without bothering us personally.

When I'm stuck in traffic, all I can think about is how long it will last and how can I get out of it. Waiting for a table in a restaurant, I focus on the anticipated words, "Mr. Stark, your table is ready." At a football game the only thing I care about is that my team wins. My whole life, my total consciousness, is contained within the walls of the stadium for that two hours. In cases like these all other facets of my life are temporarily excluded. In other words, I get intensely involved with the issue of the moment. Standing there in the dead of night, in remote wilderness, having had all of our food destroyed by bears, this tiny campsite in Yosemite National Park had my full attention. I was totally involved and I felt totally violated. For me, there was no way of dealing with it except personally. Those bears and I had been involved in a struggle over my food and they had stolen it and won. In a way, it was like burglars had broken into my home and walked out with personal property that I had worked for and earned.

Webster's Universal Unabridged Dictionary

defines *abject* as "utterly hopeless, miserable, humiliating, or wretched." For us, this was a complete and abject surrender. Never in my life had I felt so completely defeated.

At that point there was nothing more we could do but retreat to our fire and wait for daylight. We slept about four hours and did not hear anything more from the bears.

"It was like they had declared war on us and were determined, no matter what, to get all our food."

Fifteen

Wednesday morning's daylight revealed the scope of the damage. Where I live in Connecticut, we put out a large, black plastic trash bag once a week for curbside pickup. Sometimes a raccoon scratches through it and scatters a bit of garbage as it scavenges for the tasty stuff. The destruction we were looking at could easily have been the work of a dozen raccoons. Food remnants were scattered over a wide area and there was ripped packaging in random patterns between the two trees. In an ironic twist, there was a large, neat pile of bear droppings almost on top of a red plastic wrapper that once protected a round of Gouda cheese. It was almost as if the bear deliberately left his calling card with a message, "I've won and you've lost. Make no mistake about it!" I got my camera and took a picture of the two objects in their amazing juxtaposition.

That was the bad news. The good news was that the food we had dumped over the rock ledge hadn't been disturbed. Tomoko found enough to make pancakes and no one dissented when we decided that we should move on. There was no point in staying at this lovely campsite at Rancheria Falls. A dozen bears getting bolder by the day surrounded us, and our food supplies were already pretty much depleted. After finishing breakfast, we cleaned up thoroughly, packed our remaining food and equipment and broke camp by 8:30.

We still weren't ready to give up on our vacation. For some reason, each setback we encountered made us more determined to continue. Our new plan was to hike the six miles back to the junction of the Rancheria Trail with the Lake Laurel/Lake Vernon Trail and climb the steep switchbacks up and over the mountain to Lake Laurel.

Switchbacks are constructed when a mountain is very steep and too difficult for a car or person to climb straight up. They are a pattern of zigzags creating a series of hairpin turns, winding their way up the steepest grade of the mountain. Although we would have to walk more miles, the switchbacks made the grade more manageable.

After an uneventful hike to the junction, Tomoko and Jon walked another seven-tenths of a mile
to our car at Hetch Hetchy while I stayed with our
three packs. At the car they picked up the remainder
of the food that we had stored in the trunk and
rejoined me an hour and a half later. We now had a
new supply of dry cereal, raisins, juice, and other
suitable trail food. We felt rested, rejuvenated and
ready for the final segment of our trip.

We had heard that Lake Laurel was beautiful
and full of trout. In order to get there we would have
to climb the very steep mountain on a service road
built for robust four-wheel-drive maintenance vehicles. The entire length of the road was constructed in
switchbacks that were completely open to the sun.
Adding to our problems was the fact that before we
had even started the climb the temperature had
reached the high eighties. We steeled ourselves for
what promised to be the hottest, most exposed, and
steepest climb of the trip. But just as soon as we had
helped each other strap on our packs and started up
the mountain, a miracle arrived.

Each of us defines *miracles* differently. I believe
that miracles can be personal and relative. Not all of
my readers will agree that what happened next was
indeed, a miracle, but at that time, in that place, we
believed it was.

It came in the form of a pickup truck. We

heard it in the distance long before we saw it. In that relatively remote area of Yosemite National Park the sound of a vehicle was pronounced and stunning. We stopped in our tracks, turned, and waited. As soon as I saw that it was a truck, I stepped out into the road and clasped my hands together in a sign of prayer. The driver stopped. (What else would he do in a miracle-type situation!?) We explained our plight and asked if he would transport our packs to the top of the mountain. He quickly assented. Jon, gaining confidence from the driver's casual attitude, asked if we might, perhaps, accompany our packs. The amiable driver explained that this was not possible as it was a government vehicle and he wasn't allowed to give rides to people. We gratefully lifted our packs into the back of the empty truck and profusely thanked the driver for his help. He advised us that he would deposit the packs at a prominent spot just off the road at the top of the mountain.

I was thrilled that we had escaped our packs yet rather pleased that Jon's request for a ride had been rejected. I was rested and looking forward to the exercise without the packs. The hike was very demanding and hot but we were on an open road and always knew how far we had to go.

I think journeys can seem easier when we know what and where the destination is and what kind of effort it will take to get there. That doesn't mean that it may not be more interesting to take a trip into the unknown, however at that moment I was grateful for the certainty. This can be a metaphor for living. Some of us feel more confident and secure if we move from one certain stage to another. On a vacation for example, some travelers may plan all the cities, the hotels, travel in a tour bus, and be accompanied by a native guide. Others prefer more uncertainty and think that much of the fun is living on a moment-to-moment basis, enjoying the unexpected events, even difficulties, as they occur.

I can enjoy both perspectives depending on the circumstances. One of my favorite vacations occurred when my wife Cher and I combined both concepts. We bought plane tickets from New York to Zurich and return tickets from Geneva. We had never been to Switzerland and gave ourselves two weeks to get from Zurich in the center of the country to Geneva in the west with no plan of how or where we were going to spend the time in between the flights.

In this case, there in the Sierras, it took us an hour to reach the top of the mountain, a gain of 1,200 feet in elevation. We found the packs neatly stacked on a large rock at the trail intersection. It seemed like an opportune time and place for a break so we broke out our usual lunch of raisins, dried fruit, and nuts. While we were eating, a gentle old man with a large,

gnarled walking stick passed through the intersection. When he saw us his first comment was,
"Some of the longest miles in the world are in these
woods!" We liked him immediately and offered him
some of our lunch. As he sat with us he disclosed that
he had hiked on ahead but couldn't negotiate the trail
because it was too steep and difficult. He was not
happy that he was forced to turn back. We tried to
cheer him by admitting how hard it was for us too.
We told him about the pickup truck and that we had
cheated so that a three-hour trip up the switchbacks
had been cut by two-thirds. If we had had to carry
our packs to this point, there was no assurance that
we could have continued either. He left us in a more
cheerful frame of mind.

And he had been correct. We no longer had
the luxury of a maintenance road and the trail was
incredibly steep and challenging. I had to continually
look down at my feet to negotiate each step and we
had to take frequent breaks. Having the packs on our
backs again made the hike exponentially more difficult. We utilized the breaks to admire the ever-chang-
ing, always beautiful scenery. On this part of our trip
the terrain changed more than at any other time and
we appreciated the variety. The trail wound through
meadows with tall grass and wild flowers, over and
around huge boulders, through dense pine forests,
and finally into Beehive, a junction with a cold, run-

ning spring. This was the first water we had found since we had departed Hetch Hetchy, now over seven miles behind and below us. When something I take for granted is denied, it becomes very special when I obtain it. This mountain water was very special, the best we had ever experienced. It tasted, smelled, and felt clean, cold and refreshing. After gulping like insatiable animals, we replenished our canteens and bota bags and continued the remaining mile and a quarter to Laurel Lake.

Once again we were stopped in our tracks by the beauty of a Sierra lake. Laurel Lake was smaller than Cherry or Kibbe but, like them, was ringed with dense growths of dark green pines that grew to the water's edge. We were pleased to have chosen this to be our next destination and cleared a small area for a campsite not far from the edge of the water.

With setting up a tent and laying out ground cloths came the associated activity of protecting our food from the bears. We had no idea if bears were in that area, but after all we had been through, we were not about to take any chances. We knew all our previous efforts had not been successful in keeping our food out of the bears' paws, so it was important to come up with a new and better scheme.

After locating an appropriate pair of evergreens, Jon actually climbed all the way to the top of one and with considerable effort and imagination, we succeeded in suspending a bag of food 14 feet in the air and swinging at least eight feet away from either tree. This was absolutely the best that we were capable of. If the bears were successful in getting to this bag, we would still be able to get to our car in one day and that would, for all intents and purposes, be the end of our vacation.

After satisfying ourselves that our campsite was in good shape for the night, we built a fire and virtually collapsed around it. We were experiencing a general weariness, specific muscle pains, and hot, aching, blistered feet. Reflecting on the events of the day with pride, we assessed our accomplishments. We had hiked more than 16 miles with a total elevation gain of 2,600 feet, not including the many back and forths and ups and downs. In retrospect, the two steep miles the truck had hauled our packs were critical because once again, we had overestimated our ability. With our inexperience and lack of appropriate physical conditioning we shouldn't have chosen such a large expanse of ground to cover in one day. Our overconfidence came from the restful days at Rancheria Falls, where we had regained our strength, and our desire to put the bears as far behind us as possible.

Our fireside conversation naturally turned to the bears that had been such an important part of our last three days. It turned out that when we compared notes, we all really liked them. They are so clever and amazingly light on their feet for such heavy and lumbering animals. Many times, in the darkness, they had approached to within 15 feet of our campsite without our hearing them. They climbed trees only 25 feet away and we weren't aware of their presence until they were halfway up and we heard their claws gripping or slipping on the tree trunk. Thankfully, they had always left us alone personally. They were only interested in our food. And who could blame them, given the history of the park? More credit to them for their stealth, persistence, and ingenuity. In effect, they had stayed in their own habitat and had only taken advantage of food that intruders had carried in. Nevertheless we fervently hoped that we had seen the last of them.

After about an hour of rest and conversation, we prepared dinner. Unfortunately a single bear did appear, but it quickly disappeared after we banged a mess kit a few times and hurled some rocks in its direction. At just about the point where twilight turns into nighttime we discovered a bear climbing the tree where the food bag was hung. We were able to chase that one away too. It was very depressing to realize that, after all our hiking and climbing, we had not left the bears behind us. We still had to deal with them. Perhaps it was our imagination but the bears at Laurel Lake definitely seemed larger than the ones at

Rancheria Falls. It's possible that there was more food available for them at this higher elevation. In any case, Jon and I reluctantly agreed to resume our guard duty routine and each of us did have to chase an assortment of unwelcome visitors during the night.

As Thursday dawned we saw that our food was still there. To say that this was a source of deep satisfaction would be a grave understatement. To paraphrase Vince Lombardi, winning wasn't an important thing for us, it was the only thing. We had become obsessed with protecting our food. In retrospect, I think we were allowing ourselves to believe that we were learning enough outdoor lore that we were no longer mere greenhorns.

Basking in our newfound pride, we prepared a full breakfast of reconstituted juice, pancakes, and coffee. Planning a full day of rest and relaxation, we decided to explore the lake. It wasn't very large and it was easy to move from the south end to the north. There we found a long tree that had fallen into the lake. Its base was on land and the top was submerged. In between was about 40 feet of bare trunk that afforded us the opportunity to walk out over the water. We staked out this area for sunning and fishing. Tomoko stripped down to her shorts, lay with her head leaning downward toward the water, and read a paperback book. Jon walked out as far as possible and fished with our small fishing rod. As bait we had brought a nifty red and white spinner that reflected the sunlight when dragged through the water. The trout were not impressed. It didn't take us long to get bored so we continued walking around the lake until we found a sandy beach ideal for lunching and swimming.

We hadn't seen any humans since our arrival at the lake the previous afternoon, so we had a cool and cleansing nude swim after lunch. We washed ourselves to the best of our ability and didn't use soap for fear of polluting the water.

About four o'clock, Tomoko and I dropped Jon off at "our log" for more fishing while we went back to the campsite for a cup of soup. At 5:30 we returned to the log to find a dejected fisherman with an empty pot. It seems that the fish were biting but each time Jon tried to pull one in, the line wasn't strong enough. Clearly, what was needed was a landing net. No problem. I took off my long sleeve shirt and tied the sleeves. Jon and I alternated 20 minute shifts, one of us with the rod, the other with my shirt. Within an hour we had four beautiful trout flopping in the pot. Suddenly swarms of flies arrived in the area. For some reason they were very interested in, and excited about, our heads and ears, and they annoyed us to complete distraction. Then the fish seemed to lose interest in our spinner. Time to go.

Back at the campsite, Tomoko started a fire while Jon and I cleaned and gutted the trout. Over the hot coals of our wood fire, I sautéed a bit of margarine in a saucepan while Jon sliced some almonds from our lunch bags. Before long we were eating the best trout almondine ever.

After dinner we cleaned the dishes in the lake, strung up the food bag, and enjoyed the sunset as we sipped cognac from our aluminum cups. It was easy keeping the fire going with all the fallen branches in the area. No problems with the bears either that night as Jon and I alternated watches and had surprisingly little to do. The food suspension system worked again! We were becoming so confident that we even wondered if the bears thought that they had met their match, had given up on us, and had gone elsewhere.

As I lay in my tent, I noticed that the wind seemed to change direction frequently. I fell asleep listening to the rustling sound as one tree passed it to another.

"In the remaining hour of light and well into dusk we
gathered as much wood as we could for our fire..."

"...start a fire under one end of the tree, and as it burned, we would continue to push the rest of the log into the fire."

Sixteen

My prolonged exposure to the outdoors was increasing my awareness of the environment. For example, I became conscious of the habits of the bears. We had never met a bear on the trail. I didn't know where they spent the daylight hours but I guessed that they didn't have an interest in ambushing hikers. They only appeared in the late afternoon and only at our campsites where the food was more accessible than it was when it was enclosed in packs strapped to our backs. It was clear that the bears took great pains to avoid us personally while trying to get to our food.

I also learned about the daily cycles of insects. Flies enjoy sunlight and its warmth. They often settled on our nylon packs if I laid them in the sun. Mosquitoes didn't have the same interests. They appeared mostly when the sun was least intense, in the early mornings, evenings, and night. I was also fascinated by how patient mosquitoes were. If they landed on my arm or leg they took their time climbing around the hairs searching for a bit of bare skin before they inserted their proboscis to drink my blood. Ants don't seem to want to work alone. They were always involved in community projects like lifting and transporting dead insects and live vegetation to their homes. I also observed long columns of disciplined ants heading off in one direction and returning. Most of the time I wasn't able to determine their mission but I never doubted that they accomplished it. They displayed incredible strength, persistence, and determination. I thought that if humans learned to pull together like that, we'd transform the planet. Bees, too, seemed very purposeful, curiously inspecting any interesting newcomers and objects. If I didn't aggravate them they let me be and I never worried when one buzzed me. It was like they were inspecting me for something good to eat, never found it, and moved on to more promising fare.

Whenever I plan on venturing into the woods I avoid using aromatic products such as deodorant, cologne, or perfumed soap. I don't want to attract attention to myself or have a bee confuse me with a flower. On this trip it didn't seem to matter. I was easy prey for a wide variety of insects, some malevolent, some benign. I think that the novelty of having humans in the area sparked at least a modicum of curiosity and appetite stimulation.

I was able to detect which animal was in the area based on their footprints and size, shape, and texture of their skat (stools). The skat of carnivores displayed tiny, indigestible animal hairs while herbivores' droppings had a different texture. Mule deer and ground squirrels know to stay motionless to avoid detection. I had to attend Army Reserve Officer Training Corps classes in college to learn the advantages of this behavior but the animals know instinctively. I marveled at the fluidity of motion and the amazing body control that snakes possess. They have great power and grace as they swim upstream against strong currents. I also observed that trout swim near the shady bottom of a lake during the heat of the day and come to the surface to feed on flies in the early evening. That meant that the spinner we dragged near the surface was useless most of the day.

Thinking about the micro-aspects of my immediate environment led me to muse about more universal subjects. I thought about large systems like galaxies and solar systems as well as small bits and pieces like atoms. If there was life elsewhere, where was it and what was it like? And if earth hosted the only life, what was the significance of that? I wondered why planets are round and why the earth is exactly where it is. If it were closer to the sun or farther away, the delicate balance that allows life to exist would be destroyed. As for the moon, if it were closer the tides would have overrun and flooded the land yet if it were more distant, the oceans, and any possibility of life in them, would have stagnated. We take a force like gravity for granted, but I'm still left in awe about how well we are able to utilize it and how essential it is to everyday life.

If I focused on the miracle of the human body and its circulatory, respiratory, nervous, digestive, and other systems, it left me overwhelmed with appreciation and amazement; so many interrelated parts working together harmoniously! It seemed to me that we're pretty good at explaining how each system works. We don't seem to be as smart, however, in figuring out how they all came to exist and function together so efficiently in each species.

Even as I admired the beauty that's Yosemite, I despaired over our seemingly inexorable and relentless destruction of the planet. I thought of how we pollute our rivers, use the oceans for garbage and oil dumps, over fish with drift nets, clear-cut our forests, destroy the protective ozone layer with pollutants, cut down the rain forests, and on and on.

I'm still disappointed that automobile manufacturers won't make cleaner-burning cars unless offered large financial incentives or are faced with binding legislation. It's common knowledge that vehicle exhaust is one of the most significant causes of pollution on our planet. Wouldn't you think that responsible car makers would want to make vehicles with better gas mileage and cleaner exhaust systems and that drivers would want to buy them? We don't seem to resonate with the concept that we are all citizens of the world and that we all share the same irreplaceable environment.

I am, however, encouraged by three actions taken by the U. S. government in Spring 2000. On March 27 Interior Secretary Bruce Babbitt unveiled a 500 page Yosemite Valley Plan. Long in the making, it is designed to restore and protect the natural splendor of the park. It outlines a group of proposals that could cost as much as $343 million and take ten years to implement.

The placement and design of visitor facilities in Yosemite Valley date back to before the 1920s and were aimed at accommodating visitors who spent two full days driving from San Francisco and then often stayed several weeks. Now the drive takes four hours and most of the visitors don't even stay overnight. As a result the air is often heavy with automobile pollutants, the parking lots overcrowded, and the picnic areas noisy and strewn with trash.

Babbitt declared that, "This is not about turning people away from the park. The problem is not that there are too many people. The problem is there are too many cars." He stated that he hopes that in 25 to 30 years there will be no cars in the park.

His proposals include: reducing day-visitor parking spaces from about 1,500 to 550; encouraging drivers to park outside the valley and utilize new shuttle buses; tearing down several hundred cabins; destroying three bridges that restrict the flow of the Merced River and creating a 150-foot-wide protected zone along most of its length; reducing or excluding the use of snowmobiles, jet skis and tour planes; removing some roads and converting others to foot and bike trails; and restoring 180 acres of land to their natural state.

The National Park Service must approve the plan for it to go into effect but at least there are concrete proposals, submitted by a high-ranking cabinet member, to be considered.

In April 2000 the government banned the use of all personal watercraft, including Jet Skis, from the national park system.

On April 27, the Interior Department announced that the National Park Service had imposed an immediate ban on the recreational use of snowmobiles from almost all of the national parks and recreational areas. Donald J. Barry, Assistant Secretary of Interior for Fish and Wildlife and Parks stated, "Snowmobiles are noisy, antiquated machines that are no longer welcome in our national parks." It was estimated that more than 180,000 vehicles were affected. Snowmobiles are banned in Yosemite except for essential transportation.

The ban was a reaction to the petitions of over 60 environmental groups. A spokesman for the Wilderness Society said that one snowmobile can emit as many hydrocarbons and as much nitrous oxide as 1,000 cars.

How many of our extinct and endangered species can be traced to abuses by humans? I'm disturbed that we defend indefensible actions with short term, expedient answers like "jobs." I believe that we could create more jobs if we had a long-term strategy of preserving our planet and its resources but if only we had enough vision and courage to elect more enlightened members of our society to positions of power. Unfortunately we live in a country where powerful and wealthy special interests contribute large sums of money to elect politicians who respond to the contributions with quid pro quo environmentally destructive legislation. I am grateful, at least, for the legislation that sets aside and protects the national parks.

All of this past and current reflection and questioning prompts me to examine my own personal role. What should my life be about? Do I have a responsibility and, if so, to whom and for what? I would like America to have full employment but I don't want some of our workers depending on cutting down our forests or trapping dolphins in nets to earn their living. I abhor the idea of people slaughtering whales for oil or blubber, killing sharks to use only their fins, and shooting bears for their paws and gall bladders. There has to be a better way. Thinking about these questions occupied a lot of my time in Yosemite and still does.

"We had placed one large rock on each side of the fire and supported the grill on the rocks. There's something special about fish you catch and prepare yourself."

"Is that a bear over there?"

"Our first sight of the creek was a large cascading fall pouring over smooth, polished rock."

Seventeen

As soon as I exited my tent Friday morning, I was confronted by some unsettling news. Jon advised me that he wanted to abort the trip, pack everything up and return home. His reasons were not very convincing. He said that we would be leaving the next day anyway and this would mean one less night of fighting off the bears, one less night of worrying about our campfire spreading out of control, one more night of rest in a comfortable bed. This new development caught me completely by surprise. I was already disappointed that the trip would be ending the following day. I was enjoying all of our activities and relishing the beautiful, natural wilderness.

After voicing initial opposition to his idea I had to stop and think about what had motivated it. If I could figure that out, perhaps I could present an argument that might steer Jon in another direction.

My first thought was that he had enjoyed a break in the middle of the trip with a night in a hotel and a restaurant meal. That meant that he actually had spent one less day in the field than I. That led me into the realization that, although all three of us were traveling together, we were experiencing the same trip differently. Jon had gone through a day of wondering if he would ever see his wife again. That had to be harrowing, to say the least. With his self-centered approach to marriage and life, he had faced the possibility of a complete unraveling of his comfortable routine. He had also been much more emotional than Tomoko or I had been, and he had gone off the deep end on two occasions. He had shown me a side of his personality that, not only I had never seen, I had never even imagined existed. It hit me that I was interacting with a long time friend who was suddenly unpredictable. It certainly was possible that he was on the verge of a nervous breakdown. I felt that I had to tread carefully.

Jon elaborated on his proposal to Tomoko, who listened quietly and impassively. We agreed to put the issue to a vote, majority wins. That meant Tomoko would decide the matter.

Now my thoughts shifted to her. What would be her issues and what criteria would she use to decide? If she were to vote yes, let's leave now, it could, of course, be that she simply wanted to end the trip a day early. Another reason would be out of loyalty to her husband. If she voted no, it could be that, like me, she was really enjoying the trip and wanted to let it run its course. Knowing how Tomoko was developing, I thought that she might not really care about one day, more or less, but might want to demonstrate her independence from Jon. So I really had no clue as to how she would vote.

Then there was me. What was I really feeling? I had a newfound pride that I was adapting so much more easily to, what I had originally perceived as a hostile setting. I was feeling a part of an integrated ecosystem rather than being a stranger/intruder fighting off all sorts of obstacles. Problems for me at the beginning of the trip had become friendly companions or accommodations at this final stage. From a more superficial point of view, I was having fun! I also needed, and wanted, some time to wind down. I preferred a gradual natural ending instead of an abrupt, artificial termination.

Tomoko was frustratingly indecisive. She wondered aloud if we might compromise, spend the day by the lake and leave around three. That wouldn't have worked because we would have run out of daylight before we got anywhere near Kibbe Lake. She kept her own counsel for almost an hour while Jon and I kept ourselves busy with chores. Finally she said, "I guess I'd like to stay," not exactly a resounding affirmation but a vote that counted nonetheless. We stayed. Jon accepted the decision gracefully but it put a damper on the day for me, knowing how much he would have liked not to have been there. I never learned what had motivated Jon's request to end the trip or what prompted Tomoko's vote to prolong it.

We were more determined than ever to make the best of our last day. After cooking a tasty breakfast we headed for the log in the water. Jon fished, Tomoko read, and I puttered about in the woods. After we all were sufficiently bored with our activities we went to the beach at the north end of Laurel Lake for a swim and our final lunch in the woods.

Jon and Tomoko stripped and went for their last nude swim while I stayed on the shore. As luck would have it, the first humans we had seen at the lake arrived just as my friends were about to end their swim. A couple, probably in their 50s, suddenly appeared and started asking me all sorts of tourist-type questions about fishing in the area, campsites, and bears. While I politely responded, Tomoko had to ease into deeper water so her naked body was completely submerged and Jon had to be aware of where he was and come no closer.

I couldn't get rid of those people. They waved to Jon and Tomoko and yelled friendly comments that, because of the distance between them, were inaudible. The polite and efficient thing would have been for the swimmers to shorten the distance to facilitate the conversation but that wasn't possible under the circumstances. I could have told our visitors that Tomoko and Jon were naked and cold and would have liked to come out of the water but I was too embarrassed and was concerned that I couldn't say it without appearing rude. After an interminable period, we were finally left alone.

But not for long. Shortly after my friends were able to leave the water and dress, another group showed up. Funny, we had been at this site for three days and nights and had seen no one, now, within 20 minutes, two separate groups had appeared.

This new group was far more interesting than the middle-aged couple. This was a small assemblage of campers from Camp Sewanhaka, who arrived with energy and spirit to spare. There were nine boys and girls ranging in age from 11 to 15. Tom, in his twenties, was in charge and Sheila, 22, a counselor-in-training, was Tom's helper. They were excited to see us because they hadn't seen anyone in days. Gathering around us at the water's edge, they bombarded us with questions about the area, comments, wisecracks, and some of the most raunchy sexual statements, jokes and innuendoes I had ever heard. Their exuberance and spirit was refreshing even though it was a shattering interruption to our peaceful existence at that quiet spot.

One of the older girls yelled, "Let's go skinny dipping!" and I stood there amazed as the four older girls stripped off all their clothing and ran shouting and laughing into the water. Sheila quickly joined them. It was like paradise, a second Garden of Eden; five naked young women, perfectly at ease, frolicking in the pristine lake surrounded by the most beautiful scenery in the world. At that moment, in that place, there was no pretense, no facade, no status, no artificiality. I will never forget it.

After a few moments regarding their friends, the water nymphs, enjoying themselves so completely, the boys joined them in the water. Interestingly, they all wore bathing suits or underwear. I wanted to try to capture this powerful moment so after everyone had finished swimming I asked the group if I could take their picture. They thought that was a grand idea and quickly grouped themselves for the photo. Much to my surprise, the girls remained naked. When later I saw the developed picture, every one of the campers was grinning or laughing happily and naturally. It was a wonderful hour for me. I must admit that having the area filled with a variety of young, enthusiastic campers was also a major contrast and distraction from the relatively quiet days we had been spending by ourselves. If I had allowed it into my consciousness, the ebullience and boisterousness of the campers could have been an annoying interruption to the peace and serenity of Laurel Lake. Instead, it seemed so wonderful and appropriate that thoroughly natural and naive human beings could so easily blend in with and enjoy that primitive and undisturbed environment. It was a union of pristine creatures with a pristine environment. Every element seemed to belong to and fit in with every other element.

Unfortunately a reality check ended our lakeside gambol. We were out of food and needed to catch some trout if we were to eat dinner. With heavy hearts and vivid memories we gathered our fishing gear and bid adieu to the cavorting campers. Our log on the western side of the lake seemed to give us the best vantage point to the fish. It was important to take advantage of the hour between 5:30 and 6:30 when the trout seemed at least somewhat interested in a red and white spinner cast from a homemade fishing pole. This was the last hour before hordes of flies emerged from wherever flies take refuge from the intense midday heat. Fortunately it coincided with the first hour that trout seemed to become aware of stirrings of hunger and rose to the surface from the cool depths of the lake to await the advent of the flies.

Using my shirt with the knotted sleeves as a

landing net, we quickly caught five trout. Then the flies arrived and diverted the fish to an authentic banquet.

We had used the last of our margarine the previous evening but we had found an old grill that someone had discarded and we cleaned it as best we could. Jon and I scaled, gutted, and cleaned the fish. Tomoko made a wonderful fire, using the last of our wood, and we waited until the coals were white and hot. We had placed one large rock on each side of the fire and supported the grill on the rocks. This allowed us to cook the trout evenly. There's something special about fish you catch and prepare yourself. I don't know if it's our imagination or the freshness but that was the second consecutive evening that we enjoyed spectacular trout dinners.

After dinner we strung up our last food bag between trees and retreated to the campfire. We felt compelled to finish our supply of coffee and cognac and I think each of us enjoyed a special awareness of how wonderful and beautiful it was being a part of nature. There were long pauses in our conversation where we savored living in the moment. When we were ready for sleep we gathered our usual complement of bedside accouterments. Each of us went to sleep with a flashlight to locate the bear that makes the noise, a whistle to blow and Sierra cup or aluminum plate to bang, a pile of rocks to throw in the bears' direction, and a four-inch sheath knife in case it ever came to hand-to-hand combat. (That would be like trying to shoot down an F-16 jet with a BB gun but one does what one can.)

I was awakened at 1:25 a.m. by a loud crash, and woke Jon. We shined our lights around the camp perimeter but saw nothing and resumed our fitful sleep.

Upon waking when it was light, I found a large branch on the ground. Obviously a bear had been too heavy for it on its way up our food tree. Ironically, on the morning we didn't need anymore food, our bag was hanging jauntily between the trees. We tried to use up an assorted collection of left over food for breakfast, cleaned up our dishes and our campsite and set out on our 8.4 mile hike to the Hetch Hetchy Dam. Our hearts and packs were light on this final day and the route was all downhill. It took us only three and a half hours and we arrived at 12:45. The last four miles sped by as we were joined by the nymphs from Camp Sewanhaka who again supplied us with incredibly racy conversation. Surprisingly the most disgusting comments came from assistant counselor Sheila. At the time it was funny and welcome but upon further reflection I thought adults in a supervisory position with children should exercise more restraint and judgment.

It was a major relief to see the car where we

had left it, with no damage and full tires. It felt great to shed our boots and extra pair of wool socks and change into comfortable driving clothes. We had left sneakers in the car and putting them on after 15 days in heavy boots made my feet feel like they were flying. Before long we were driving through the oppressive 100 degree heat and dry wind of the San Joaquin Valley. We stopped for cold sodas in bottles, burgers cooked from fresh beef, and watermelon. Twice more we paused for cold sodas trying to quench a seemingly insatiable thirst for cold liquids.

When we finally arrived at Jon's and Tomoko's home, we unpacked the car and headed for the scale. We knew we had all lost weight but wanted to know how much. Tomoko had lost seven pounds from 123 to 116, Jon lost ten pounds from 168 to 158 and I was the big loser (or winner?), losing 15 pounds from 180 to 165. I know lots of people who would like to lose this much in about two weeks. Would you like to lose eight percent of your weight in two weeks and still be healthy? I was quite pleased. The surprising aspect of this weight loss was that we had eaten well and in good quantity. All dinners were generous portions for three people, and all breakfasts and dinners had multiple courses. It proved, for us, the benefit of exercise. We felt leaner and more shapely than before we left so we made liberal use of the camera to record how trim we could look when we worked at it. Unfortunately as soon as I resumed my normal life style I regained the weight.

The next activity could be described as the big cleanup. The first priority was ourselves. I had taken many showers in my life, but the one I took that evening was truly amazing. Streams of black dirt that flowed from my body meandered along the bottom of the white tub slowly making its way to the drain. Each time I washed another part of my body I unleashed more rivulets of black dirt. It was fascinating to watch and seemed endless. I don't think I've ever enjoyed a shower so much.

Shaving a two-week growth of beard was more traumatic. I sort of admired the visible sign of my outdoor activities and could have talked myself into believing that I had transformed myself into an outdoorsman. The face I regarded in the mirror, however, did not reflect a successful businessman. The problem was that in a few days I would have to revert to my National Sales Manager role and what I then considered my new rugged look would be perceived by my customers and the company president as an unkempt executive who should have known how to take better care of his appearance. Two weeks' growth could never have passed for a beard. I looked more ratty than rugged. Not shaving was not an option.

I didn't discuss these reflections with Jon and

Tomoko but I knew that we all felt much better being clean. It took us quite a while to scour the cooking pots and mess kits and it was a real luxury to toss our clothes into a washing machine. As much as I enjoy living in the wilderness, I don't discount the benefits of modern conveniences.

As the washing machine droned on, we were finally able to sit in the Roberts' living room and review the adventures of the past two exciting weeks. We had learned so much about ourselves, each other, and about living in harmony with nature. Despite the mistakes we had made we were proud of our physical accomplishments and field ingenuity. It would never have occurred to us two weeks earlier that we would be climbing trees to suspend food bags or throwing rocks at a dozen wild bears. I'm not so sure however, that all of us were as proud of what we had learned about our own psychological make-up. I certainly had lost a great deal of respect for Jon. Before the trip, I had admired him but disagreed with some of his ideas. Now I discovered that I no longer admired him. Under pressure he had behaved selfishly and wasn't able to exercise even adequate self-control. For me, it was with a complex set of mixed feelings that we ended the Sierra part of our vacation.

Part 4
Friends

"We started our hike by crossing the dam...and then proceeded up the lovely terraces of the reservoir."

Eighteen

The next evening Jon and Tomoko took me to the Los Angeles Airport for my flight home. The three of us hugged tightly and expressed the warmest of personal thoughts and feelings.

As the plane carried me through the darkness that separated Los Angeles from New York I finally felt comfortable exploring doubts that had plagued me for weeks before and during the hike. The events of the trip itself had actually resolved all questions for me. Jon's urgings for me to have sex with Tomoko before the vacation had not, after all, been an impediment to the complex relationships that the three of us shared. I had barely even thought of it during the trip. The subject only surfaced, and then, only in my mind, when we went swimming in the nude and those occasions were few and far between.

Having just put ourselves into the intimate setting of our two-week wilderness trip, I believe that Tomoko and I learned that there was no hint of a sexual attraction for each other. At least that's what I was thinking on the plane.

Subsequently, I learned that I had misjudged Tomoko's state of mind. Several months later, when she and I were having lunch together, she asked me, if she were to divorce Jon would I marry her? I was shocked by the question and realized how fragile she and her marriage were. At the time I was very involved with a woman who was to become my wife and I used that as an excuse to tell Tomoko that I wouldn't be available to her for marriage. I was happy to have an excuse to avoid the subject of, what I considered to be, our total incompatibility. Her question led me to believe that she had stayed in the marriage with Jon because she hadn't been able to find a suitable substitute and didn't want to be alone, particularly while raising her children. Score one for the efficacy of Jon's idea of the economically efficient, passionless marriage.

I hope Tomoko got a modicum of personal satisfaction a year or so later when she quietly told me that she was glad we had not had the relationship that Jon had suggested. That too was a surprise because I knew she had wanted to please Jon.

My relationship with Tomoko had barely changed during the event-filled two-week vacation. Because Jon was always present, Tomoko had been quiet, reserved, and generally agreeable. She did crack once after she and Jon returned to my campsite and while looking for the boys and their mule train, couldn't locate the trail. At the time I actually thought that her emotional letdown was quite normal given all that she had been through. True, I had never seen her lose control of herself before but neither had I been with her during such a time of stress. I think most people would have had similar reactions of despair and hopelessness under the same circumstances. I was disappointed that she hadn't shown the same decisiveness on the trail that she routinely demonstrated at work and when alone with me. I did, however, recognize that Jon's presence changed the dynamics for her in a significant way.

My relationship with Jon, on the other hand, had seriously deteriorated. I found his behavior repugnant when he thought Tomoko might have died. I know a few people who are totally self-centered and think the world revolves around themselves but they are not my friends. I don't respect people who spend their lives manipulating others to serve themselves and this is what Jon was doing. Before this trip I had never seen it so clearly.

Often the same kind of thing happens when a happily married couple starts a business together. At home they are convinced they know everything about their spouse but in a work environment they display patterns of behavior that neither had seen before. It's often enough to end the relationship.

I have a simple philosophy vis-a-vis friendships. My moment on earth is finite. It will end on some indeterminate date. During the days I have here, I have the ability to choose how I will spend my time. That implies a choice of whom I will spend it with. The often quoted line from II Corinthians, "For ye suffer fools gladly, seeing yourselves as wise." triggers a thought. This in turn causes me to focus on the word fool. Who do I consider a fool? If I want to give meaning to my life, I can't waste it and I don't have a lot of time for "fools."

Although it is clear that all of us have many qualities and behavior patterns, each of us cannot be expected to appreciate all of them in every person we meet. In this context, I generally avoid people who are self-obsessed or totally negative. I don't like to spend time with people who talk without listening or complain without seeing the positive. Instead of being with the proverbial people who curse the darkness, I gravitate to people who turn on the light. I don't have the time or energy to be close friends with everyone who passes my way.

A change in one's environment can often become a catalyst for enhancing relationships. In the late 1990s I lived and taught in Herefordshire, England. One of the most important influences on my life there was my friendship with the artists, David and Liz Lovegrove. In moving to a small, rented cottage in a remote rural hamlet near the Welsh border, I was compelled to leave material belongings behind. My possessions gathered over a lifetime stayed in the United States, however I couldn't avoid taking all of my emotional and psychological baggage with me.

Just as it is not possible for any of us to take just a portion of our DNA on a trip, so it is not possible to divide or eliminate our ingrained emotional baggage.

That aside, I was inadvertently given the opportunity to recreate myself for that move. Often referred to as "the American teacher" by locals, I was warmly welcomed by them, and friendships formed quickly and easily.

David, Liz, and the others had no conception of my being born in New York City, had not and would not have the occasion to meet my parents, other relatives, and American friends. They knew nothing of my past unless I chose to disclose it.

The friendship that the Lovegroves and I

forged started with our shared interests of music and art. We accepted each other for what we were in the present, not what we had done in the past.

The friendship was enhanced by their introducing me to the local culture, which was totally different from anything I had experienced in the United States. When the Lovegroves and I went out in the evening, it was to go country dancing or to share the table of local artisans. Daytime hours were filled with lessons of the English countryside, such as how to care for sheep and how to pluck chicken feathers. On one occasion I was studiously drilled in the techniques of shooting pheasants. When my first day for shooting arrived, I had the most beautiful bird in the sights of my borrowed shotgun. It was enormous and seemed to fly towad me in slow motion, but I couldn't bring myself to pull the trigger.

The Lovegroves also introduced me to homespun arts and crafts, making and painting earthenware and stoneware, assembling totems, and painting local landscapes and still lifes. Their sharing of these experiences was exciting for me and helped cement our friendship. Now when I'm with David and Liz, we have conversations about subjects completely different than I have with anyone else.

Edward Elgar, the English composer, was also

born and lived much of his life in Herefordshire. It's difficult to be interested in music and reside in that area without being exposed to his story and music.

In 1899 he wrote *Variations on an Original Theme*, which is better known as the *Enigma Variations*. He composed 14 short variations and attributed each of them to his wife and 13 close friends, inscribing their respective initials on each. Since I became familiar with the piece, I sometimes play a little personal game and think of my friends and acquaintances in musical terms. I identify each with a work, key, instrument, rhythm, tempo, or volume.

For example, my wife is a symphony in the key of C major. That key has no black notes and is always bright and clear. She's a symphony because she's complex and multifaceted, embracing many themes. There are many different melodies, rhythms and sonorities to her personality. Since she interfaces with many people in her job, has numerous friends, and is always active and accomplishing something, I think of her life tempo as allegro. She always sees the positive side of an issue and is unfailingly enthusiastic. In my view, she never modulates out of a major key. I associate her with the warm, rich, full mellow tones of a cello.

Tomoko, on the other hand, is a sonata in a minor key. A minor interval in music is smaller than a major interval by a chromatic half-step and creates a more mournful sound. She's never ebullient and seems to diminish herself in self-effacing movements and quiet conversation. She reminds me of the undertones of a bass violin. Like the bass, she rarely demonstrates enthusiasm, but is a wonderful support and accompaniment. Her rhythm rarely changes and is pretty much predictable. Every orchestra needs bass violins.

Jon is really more than one opus. His mercurial personality can lead him into major or minor mode on any given day. He is complex, leading me to think of a major work with a multitude of movements in various keys, played at varying volumes. His is an instrument with a wide range. When we first lost Tomoko on the trail, he wailed and moaned, reminding me of a saxophone playing the blues. When he's happy, he can be a violin playing joyfully in its upper ranges.

Having seen the darker side of Jon on the trail, I felt my respect rapidly slipping away. He had always been emotionally inaccessible but I had admired his mind and relished our discussions and arguments. Now, the liabilities started to exceed the assets.

In the United States, I teach an adult education course on investing. I suggest that my students periodically review their portfolios to decide what ratio of stocks to bonds is appropriate for them and to do some maintenance. I also inquire if they currently own the best possible stocks. I ask them whether they would buy these same stocks today, and if not, might they be better off selling them and using the money to buy others?

Friendships certainly are different from stocks, but without being callous, I decided to employ a similar philosophy with respect to relationships. A major tenet of Equity Theory is that each person in a relationship must feel that he or she is giving and receiving equal benefit if both are to be fulfilled. If one believes that he is giving more than the other it can raise at least two problems. If I perceive that I give more to the relationship than you, I might resent you for not providing your fair share. If you feel you are receiving more than you are giving, it may lead to feelings of guilt. People in relationships often walk fine, almost indistinguishable, lines. Marriage and friendships are often very tenuous relationships that depend on constant attention, work, and compromise.

I've devoted some time to thinking about my friendships. I discovered that some old friends were no longer contributing anything positive to my life nor I to theirs. I realized that I was dragging a few along only because we had shared a long history. But in time we had outgrown each other or evolved in different directions with dissimilar interests. I was al-

allowing them to distract me from spending my time more valuably.

I feel cleansed and revitalized letting some relationships go and making efforts to rekindle others. In being proactive, I'm making my life more fulfilling.

I also realized that I had enjoyed friendships around the world that I had allowed to languish that I now wanted to renew. Perhaps I wasn't able to appreciate them sufficiently earlier or hadn't worked hard enough to overcome geographical obstacles. I decided to perform some maintenance on my own portfolio, as it were. I made a few phone calls and wrote several letters in an attempt to make some dates with those I hadn't seen in a while. Our social calendar was filled with "new" people in the next few months.

Independently of me, my wife seemed to be pursuing the same course of action based on her experiences at her high school reunion. She organized meetings with school friends she hadn't seen in 35 years. Now she's traveling all around the country meeting with "girl friends" she hasn't seen in decades. She's finding the "new" friendships even more vital and fun than they were in school.

A college fraternity brother phoned to tell me that when he goes to reunions, some of the people he wants to see don't come, and a number of people he doesn't care about do. So he tracked down all the brothers from our class and the classes immediately before and after ours. He then invited 40 of us to lunch in New York City. Out of the 40 men, 28 came and had an incredible time. We vowed to organize our own reunion every year, sharing the expenses and visiting various venues.

I had an interesting lunch with a friend of mine not long ago. He told me that we would always be friends because once two people had discovered personal traits that drew them to each other, they would never lose the tie. If the positive characteristics were strong enough to create a friendship in the first place, they would be there forever. Because of his theory he felt an obligation to try to retain friendships with everyone he had ever befriended and he found himself having to stretch quite a lot.

I argued that if his theory were true, we wouldn't need the word *divorce* in our vocabulary. People live dissimilar lives and have different experiences and personal contacts. If each of us is evolving as we live, we don't necessarily evolve in the same way or at the same rate. The Yosemite hike can be seen as a metaphor for life. If life is a journey, we don't all walk the same trail at the same pace and we don't all seek the same destination.

In college my friends shared the same problems and interests with me. Now we have gone on to lead our own lives, no longer having the unifying college-type problems to bind us together. Our interests are often quite disparate. No relationship can be absolutely perfect but as long as the benefits outweigh the liabilities, the relationship might endure.

One's perceptions of the benefits and liabilities can also change. I remember a previous friendship where the positives were finally eclipsed by the negatives. My friend suddenly started a pattern of arriving very late to appointments, was insensitive to my issues, and became mean and sarcastic. He blamed it on stress at work, but it was no longer fun to be around him. I tried to help him deal with the work situation by repeatedly offering sympathy and suggestions but he rejected them and seemed to wallow in his misery as he became angrier and angrier. He also became emotionally inaccessible. I phoned him less and less and finally not at all.

Obviously I'm expressing opinions and feelings about my own relationships. Each of my friends and acquaintances has his or her own feelings about me in particular and about relationships in general. Although I have tried and continue to strive to be a good friend, I know I fail to varying degrees. In fact, I fall short to some extent in every relationship. My real friends don't hesitate to respectfully tell me how I can better satisfy their needs. If I can't be responsive over a reasonable time, and they find me a more negative than positive influence in their lives, then I'm not surprised if they move on.

These kinds of thoughts made the six-hour trip literally fly by. As I pushed up my little shade and looked out the window, I noticed that the clusters of lights below were larger, nearer, and much brighter. We were approaching New York.

As we descended I wondered again if my backpack, checked by the airline, would arrive intact, in tatters or at all.

We crossed over the Hudson River on the way into Kennedy Airport and I stared at the lights of the George Washington Bridge. They seemed to illuminate something in the distant recesses of my mind.

It was a major relief, ten minutes later, to see my bright orange backpack serpentining on the baggage conveyor belt.

Nineteen

Tomoko telephoned me in New York about a month after the vacation, wondering if she might write to me. She felt that writing her most personal thoughts might help her to better understand who she was and what she wanted. The arrangement was to be one-sided, I was to read her letters but not respond. Jon was never to know about the correspondence.

It was as if Tomoko wanted to put herself on the psychiatrist's couch and expose her most intimate thoughts without risking any critical response from the psychiatrist. Since I didn't have any role to play or any responsibility to fulfill, it wasn't a problem for me, so I agreed. Besides, I lived alone and was always happy to receive mail.

She wrote to me for about 14 months. At first the letters came twice a week, at the end it was more like twice a month. From the tone I was sure that the decrease in frequency was due more to her accommodation with her lifestyle than her boredom with letter writing. The more her daily activities distracted her from her marital problems, the less she felt the need to articulate them. As her children matured and spent more time away from home, she had less and less to do with Jon and household duties and her life became simpler. She even joined a bridge club and a book discussion group where she blossomed.

Jon and Tomoko and I exchanged Christmas cards and letters for several years after our Sierra vacation. But we haven't been in touch in the last three or four years.

I'm convinced this mutual evolution of our relationship is the best resolution for all of us.

Twenty

It wouldn't surprise me to learn that while reading this book some readers might have asked themselves questions like, "Why would relatively sane people deliberately put themselves in harm's way? Why expose themselves to rattlesnakes, dangerous terrain, hungry bears, hordes of biting and stinging insects, and hypothermia, when they could enjoy a nice quiet vacation curled up on a beach with a good book and a piña colada?" It is true that my friends and I could have died or been severely injured on this vacation so I must admit that those are reasonable questions given the circumstances. Not surprisingly my friends and relatives have raised similar questions many times. In fact, I have asked myself the same things in order to promote self-understanding.

As important as it is for me to give a positive spin to my life, both for my own sanity and for others' understanding and respect, it's more important to be honest with myself. My mother once told me that she thought that I have a "death wish" because of all the dangerous activities to which I have eagerly exposed myself. When I heard her words I dismissed them out of hand as absurd, but they have lingered in my consciousness and bothered me continually. I didn't want them to be true because they implied that I might not be happy with myself or the life I was living.

In order to avoid being bothered by the idea that I might have a death wish, I have engaged in considerable introspection and self-examination. I believe that I have come up with an honest evaluation, and after all the work and time I have devoted to it, I'm surprised at its relative simplicity.

I covet insecurity and personal challenge because I believe that self-discovery, personal growth, and fulfillment cannot be truly achieved by living a comfortable and complacent life. This Yosemite vacation was just what I needed to put myself into challenging physical, psychological, and emotional situations where I was able to discover and grow and consequently move forward to the fulfillment of my life's goals.

When I look into my past it is easy to see where my search for insecurity originated. Born in the United States to parents who were educated and reasonably financially self-sufficient, I have always been handed the material possessions I needed. I went to good schools and was fortunate enough to be given music, dance, and Sunday School lessons, as well as being sent to after-school play groups and summer camps.

After attending an Ivy League university I went into active military service where I became an officer. I was able to call most of my own shots within a large and complex organization that had the means, facilities, and personnel to help me solve any problem that might have arisen. Being called "Sir" and saluted by enlisted men added to my self-satisfaction. Immediately after leaving military service I was able to obtain employment and was never unemployed for long. In my work I was always successful and was rewarded for my accomplishments. During my entire lifetime I've had everything I needed or wanted. I've felt comfortable and complacent.

Beneath the surface, however, I wasn't really satisfied. During my 33 years of employment I continually felt that my life needed a shaking up. My last 15 years of corporate employment, I worked for a large company that had many divisions devoted to employee comfort and well being. If I had a medical or dental problem, there was a comprehensive medical plan. If an emotional or psychological problem surfaced I could call a toll free number and a trained social worker would counsel me. All my expenses at company meetings were paid for and airline tickets arrived in the mail before I departed. If I had to relocate, those expenses were covered too and if I couldn't sell my house quickly, the company sold it for me. There were ergonomic advisors who advised me on selecting a desk chair for posture and comfort and lamps for relief of eyestrain. Days later the furniture arrived at my house paid for in full. Even many of my job assignments were relatively user friendly as the company downloaded spreadsheets to my computer and I simply filled in the blanks.

Many will read this and think how lucky I was and wonder why I was discontented. And it's true, I was incredibly fortunate and was well aware of it. I never stopped appreciating working for employers who were concerned about their employees and who implemented policies to take care of them. Nevertheless, the more time went by the more restless I became. I wanted to be more creative, to not have everything handed to me as it had been during my childhood. I wanted to go out on a limb, to take risks, to be allowed to fail and learn how to deal with that failure. In essence, I wanted to find out who I was, what I was capable of doing, and where I fell short.

A large calendar attached to my refrigerator

displayed a month at a time. When January arrived I wrote numbers in descending order on each day of the next 12 months showing how many days there were to the date of my eligibility for early retirement. I gave a month's notice 30 days before that date arrived.

Within six months I was living in France precisely because I didn't know anyone there, was looking for a job but had little prospect of finding one, and could barely speak the language. I wanted to shake up my life to obtain the one thing I had never been able to have: insecurity.

It didn't take long for me to recognize that self-discovery was in proportion to how much insecurity I felt. Having had everything handed to me, I had never been really challenged and had no idea how I would react in adverse circumstances.

The trip to Yosemite was a perfect antidote for self-ignorance and self-doubt. In the short space of two weeks I was confronted with a unique variety of challenges that required quick, instinctive responses. There was no way that I could have practiced ahead of time, no way to have learned appropriate behavior.

When Jon and Tomoko collapsed on the trail and gave up all hope, I was resolute and took control. Would I have been as strong if I had been alone, or did I take command because it was a matter of survival and there was no one else to do it? I can never know the answers, but if I had not put myself into the situation I would never have had the opportunity to face the problem and deal with it. Many years later I am still proud as I look back at the incident and recall how I reacted.

This reminds me of something that occurred during the first week of my first job. I was on the Executive Training Squad at R. H. Macy and Co. and was performing stock work on the sales floor. A customer suddenly fell to the floor and twitched uncontrollably. My colleagues all headed in the opposite direction. I ran to her, pulled her tongue out of her throat, put my pen in her mouth to prevent her from swallowing her tongue, and comforted her until professional help arrived. It was a very uncomfortable situation for me while it was happening but 40 years later I still remember it with pride. I needed difficult situations like that to enhance my self-understanding and self-esteem. My experiences in Yosemite were made to order.

The most important lesson I learned in the Sierras is that there are existing environments continually functioning by themselves without my presence. I am a minute element of a huge and complex universe. Wherever I am, it is up to me to adapt to the environment, not the other way around. Nature is doing just fine and doesn't need me to interfere with it in any way. There is a natural harmony in the world that I must connect myself to if I am to live at peace. Would I have learned this if I had stayed home or vegetated on a beach?

I hated the hordes of aggressive mosquitoes, feared the hungry bears, and if given the choice would have assiduously avoided spending days alone on a mountaintop. But on a subconscious and spiritual level I think I knew that at that time in my life, that was where I wanted and needed to be.

By consciously uprooting myself from my comfort zones, I created a much more interesting life. I positioned myself to enrich my experiences and co-incidentally learn a variety of life's lessons.

Each experience added to the foundation of my persona and provided a new level on which to build. It was the boredom and comfort level of my job that prompted me to venture into the Sierras. The resulting experiences enabled me to grow in confidence to the point where I was able to live in France and deal with the inevitably dissimilar challenges there. Understanding and learning from the difficulties I had to deal with in my first marriage helped me prepare for my second.

Am I unique in having these thoughts? Not at all. Many of us have a modicum of boredom or complacency in our lives and some of us are unsettled by it. I think that many can identify with growing in the face of difficulty although not everyone will actively search for a challenge. Sometimes we need to wait until the itch reaches a certain level of irritability before we are prompted to scratch. I am merely presenting my point of view as a means of raising the issue and providing a reference point for others to relate to their own life experiences.

To be honest, I didn't confront the Sierra Nevada Mountains simply to encounter hardships for personal growth. That would be a gross oversimplification and a bit pretentious. My second motivation was that I simply wanted to have fun, to have a good time. I like hiking, sleeping in a tent or under the stars, cooking over an open fire, and drinking pure, cold, mountain spring water. I take pleasure participating in all the outdoor activities that are associated with this kind of trip. At home I jog, walk, and swim because I like feeling the elements of my body working and the way I feel and look afterwards. I enjoy being in the fresh air, deeply inhaling and exhaling.

I have an affinity for nature and am exhilarated when I'm outdoors. When I lived in Santa Monica, I was a sunset groupie, going to the Palisades every evening to watch the sun set in the most western part of the continental United States. I mar-

veled at the changing hues, the subtlety of the shad-
ings, and the rapid changes of each sunset.

When I'm outdoors I feel closer to God. I
recognize my relatively infinitesimal size in the universe and it helps me shed my destructive ego for the
moment. It's as far as I can get from being called Sir
by a saluting soldier. Being in the wilderness literally
is awe-inspiring and I love the feeling.

These two reasons, wanting to create oppor-
tunities for personal growth and enjoying the outdoors, convince me that rather than having a death
wish, I have a definite propensity to enhancing and
enriching my life. Improving myself is a major
goal—I try to be a better person today than I was
yesterday. A hiking trip, at the very least, holds the
promise of physical exercise and conditioning and
that, by itself, is sufficient reason to make the trip.

Sharing time with friends is another obvious
motive for taking a wilderness trip. We are all so
caught up with the day-to-day details that make up
our lives that it takes a special effort to reserve a significant amount of time to be with people who are
equally busy. Once away from our normal and comfortable settings we are free to interact and let our
relationships lead into fresh and often surprising patterns. In uncommon surroundings we tend to share
new experiences, friendships are free to ebb and flow.

Often new dimensions and boundaries to our relationships are forged.

I have attended many off-site executive meetings because companies I have worked for wanted to promote personal interactions that would be less inhibited than those in ordinary business environments. The company presidents I have worked with believed that communication would be more forthcoming and honest in a hotel meeting room at a resort than in the president's office or a boardroom. Taking friendships "on the road" for an extended period of time can have the same results.

This was another reason I took the trip with Tomoko and Jon, and although our relationship resulted in more ebbing than flowing, it was worth the experience of probing another level beneath the familiar surface. I believe that the deeper we delve the more authentic we become. Superficial, when applied to friendships, has a pejorative connotation.

My Sierra story has ended. When I reflect on the Yosemite adventures I encountered I wonder: Would I take a major hiking trip in the Sierras today? When I try to respond to my own question I find myself firmly planted on the proverbial fence. On one side is a definite "maybe," on the other, a "probably not."

If I did go, the knowledge and experience I've

acquired would certainly lead me into planning a shorter trip, both in duration and total miles. I've also learned it would be wiser to hike fewer miles each day. And if I did it again I would factor in elevation gain and loss as well as linear miles. On a shorter trip I wouldn't need so much "stuff" so I could carry a significantly lighter pack. As much as I enjoyed being with the bears, I would now look to avoid them. I would take the trip in a season when mosquitoes are dormant. Physical conditioning would be high on my list of preparatory activities. If the physical demands were daunting then, they would be insurmountable now. Shortening the mileage, lightening the load, and being in better shape would go a long way to making such a trip more manageable and enjoyable. Finally, I would look for companions who had survival skills or hiking experience, people I could rely on. I didn't want to be the leader then and have no interest in taking on the responsibilities now.

As I've matured and lived my life, I no longer need to test myself against the elements. I'm more comfortable with who I am. The benefits of my Sierra story included facing and dealing with difficulties that led to a life-transforming experience. I'm thinking that, for my next life-transforming experience, I might see what happens if I park myself in a comfortable lounge chair next to my wife on a quiet beach with a piña colada in one hand and a good adventure story in the other.

Henry B. Stark

About the Author

Henry B. Stark was born June 5, 1937, in New York City. In 1959, he graduated from Cornell University with a B.A. in Philosophy and served as an officer in the U.S. Army Artillery at Fort Sill, Oklahoma, and Fort Dix, New Jersey. He has been Vice President of Sales and Marketing and National or Regional Sales Manager for several men's branded apparel companies during his 33-year business career. At Levi Strauss & Co., he was named Salesman of the Year twice, once for the east-coast market, once for the national market.

He and his wife Cher owned and operated a French home-stay program for a number of years, matching American and Canadian families with host families with similar interests throughout France.

Stark lived in England and France, where he taught a variety of business courses at the college level. In his years in France, he lectured regularly at Centre Audiovisuel de Royan pour l'Etude des Langues near Bordeaux and taught business courses at the Institut Supérieure de Gestion et de Commerce in Tours. He was awarded the Diplôme d'Études en Langue Française from the Ministere de l'Éducation Nationale, République Française. He has also worked for government-sponsored agencies in Europe, counseling unemployed businessmen and business executives of small firms.

Stark has also taught college students in the United States for more than 20 years. He has lectured at the Yale, Cornell, and University of Hartford graduate business schools and has taught business courses in a wide variety of programs in New England. He has developed and presented conferences in both marketing and investing in the U.S. and Great Britain.

Since 1996, he has had more than a dozen articles published in a variety of magazines in the United States and Great Britain.

An enthusiastic outdoorsman, he has canoed the Allagash, Kennebic, and Dead Rivers in Maine, as well as canoeing and rafting white water rivers in Tennessee, Pennsylvania, Connecticut, Delaware, New York, and California. Besides hiking in California's Yosemite National Park, he has climbed mountains in another half-dozen states. While living in Maine, he served as a ranger on the public trails at The Wells National Estuarine Research Reserve. Although in retirement, he remains active by walking three miles a day, swimming laps several times a week, and cross-country skiing when there is snow.

Henry Stark has been married to Cher Powell for 18 years and has two daughters, Susan and Beth, by a previous marriage.

Further Reading

Adult, Young Adult

Adams, Ansel, Stillman, Andrea G. (editor), *Yosemite*. Boston: Little Brown & Company, 1995.

Adams, Ansel, Stillman, Andrea G. (editor), Szarkowski, John (illustrator). *Yosemite and the High Sierra*. Boston: Little Brown & Company, 1994.

Browning, Peter. *Yosemite Place Names: The Historic Background of Geographic Names in Yosemite National Park*. Great West Books, 1988.

Cameron, Robert W., Gillman, Harold (photographer). *Above Yosemite*. Cameron & Co., 1983.

Clyde, Norman (photographer), Benti, Wynne (editor), Wright, Cedric (photographer). *Close Ups of the High Sierra*. Bishop, California: Spotted Dog Press, 1998.

Duane, Timothy P. *Shaping the Sierra: Nature, Culture, and Conflict in the Changing West*. Berkeley, California: University of California Press, 1999.

Felzer, Ron. *Hetch Hetchy.* Berkeley, California: Wilderness Press, 1992.

Freeman, Charlotte McGuinn. *Place Last Seen: A Novel*. New York: Picador, 2000.

Graydon, Charles K. *Trail of the First Wagons over the Sierra Nevada*. Tucson, Arizona: Patrice Press, 1994.

Guyton, Bill. *Glaciers of California: Modern Glaciers, Ice Age Glaciers, Origin of Yosemite Valley, and a Glacier Tour in the Sierra Nevada*. Berkeley, California: University of California Press, 1998.

Harvey, H. Thomas. *The Sequoias of Yosemite National Park*. El Portal, California: Yosemite Association, 1988.

Howard, Thomas Frederick. *Sierra Crossing: First Roads to California*. Berkeley, California: University of California Press, 1998.

Johnston, Hank. *The Yosemite Grant, 1864-1906*. El Portal, California: Yosemite Association, 1995.

King, Clarence, Farquhar, Francis P. (editor). *Mountaineering in the Sierra Nevada*. Lincoln, Nebraska: University of Nebraska Press, 1997.

Krist, John. *50 Best Short Hikes in Yosemite and Sequoia/Kings Canyon.* Berkeley, California: Wilderness Press, 1993.

Medley, Steven P. *The Complete Guidebook to Yosemite National Park.* El Portal, California: Yosemite Association, 1998.

Moore, James G. *Exploring the Highest Sierra.* Stanford: Stanford University Press, 2000.

Muir, John. *Our National Parks.* Madison, Wisconsin: University of Wisconsin Press, 1981.

Muir, John, Engberg, Robert, Wesling, Donald. *To Yosemite and Beyond: Writings from the Years 1863-1875.* Salt Lake City: University of Utah Press, 1999.

Olmsted, Frederick Law. *Yosemite and the Mariposa Grove: A Preliminary Report, 1865.* El Portal, California: Yosemite Association (reissue), 1995.

Roper, Steve. *Recollections of a Yosemite Rockclimber.* Seattle: Mountaineers Books, 1998.

Sargent, Shirley. *Enchanted Childhoods: Growing Up in Yosemite.* Flying Spur Press, 1993.

Secor, R. J. *The High Sierra: Peaks, Passes, and Trails.* Seattle: Mountaineers Books, 1992.

Schaffer, Jeffrey P. *The Geomorphic Evolution of the Yosemite Valley and Sierra Nevada Landscapes: Solving the Riddles in the Rocks.* Berkeley, California: Wilderness Press, 1997.

Swedo, Suzanne. *Hiking Yosemite National Park.*
     Helena, Montana: Falcon Publishing, 2000.
Wuerthner, George. *Yosemite: A Visitor's Companion.*
     Mechanicsburg, Pennsylvania: Stackpole
     Books, 1994.

Children

San Souci, Robert D., San Souci, Daniel R.
     (illustrator). *Two Bear Cubs: A Miwok Legend
     from California's Yosemite Valley.* El Portal,
     California: Yosemite Association, 1997,
Siebert, Diane, Minor, Wendell (illustrator). *Sierra.*
     New York: Harper Collins Publishers, 1991
Stirling, Ian, Lang, Aubrey (photographer). *Bears:
     Sierra Club Wildlife Library.* San Francisco:
     Sierra Club Books for Children, 1995.
Tesar, Jenny E. *America's Top 10 National Parks.*
     Woodbridge, Connecticut: Blackbirch Press,
     1998

Index